∞ DAWN N. BOYLAND ∞

A Year In Thought: God's Whispers

Dawn N. Boyland

© 2010 – 2015 by Dawn N. Boyland and Equally Yoked Heavenly Creations Services; All Rights Reserved; Library of Congress Certificate of Registration Number: **TXu 1-707-803**

ISBN-10 0-578-06878-7

ISBN-13 978-0-578-06878-7

This Trade Paperback Original is published by:

Equally Yoked Heavenly Creations Services

Irving, Texas 75039

eyhcs2010@gmail.com

This is a collection of poetry and prose regarding the author's personal journey and intimate reflection time with the Holy Spirit during the first eight months of 2010.

To order copies of this book please contact the author at

eyhcs2010@gmail.com, visit www.amazon.com, or any other

commonly known bookstore.

Credits

Editor: Dawn N. Boyland

Cover Design By: Nosae Designs

Printing Company: Create Space

Equally Yoked Heavenly Creations Services

EYHCS

A YEAR IN THOUGHT:

GOD'S WHISPERS

By

Dawn N. Boyland

A Thought from the Author

Learning to step out on faith means having the

courage to walk by faith and not by natural sight

in a time when everything around you says, I

can't …yet, with God you saying I can and

proving I am, by your walk, because HE is all you

are not.

You will know them by their Fruit.

Matthew 7:16

Acknowledgement

Above all, I acknowledge you Heavenly Father to whom I had the joy, pleasure, and blessing to be the first to read the whispers of your heart. They restored me from pieces into your humble servant. I give all the glory to you for accomplishing in me what man could not, which is the restoration of a sound mind, body, and spirit. It is a battle I laid before you on the throne and you covered by the blood of Jesus.

This is a special acknowledgement to Nelson Eason, owner of Nosae Designs' the artist of this book cover, friend, and brother in Christ who walked me through the finishing touches of God's masterpiece. Had God not sent him at the time he did the product in your hand would not be as it has become.

A special acknowledgement to Betty Warner who spoke this book into fruition alongside of me in the midst of my storm at the beginning of this year; we sat on her patio, as everything around we appeared broken she reminded me when I could not remind myself of the amazing and sustaining power of God.

An acknowledgement to my sister, Elizabeth Turner who stood by me at times most others would have strayed away. Thank you for joining me in a quest for success. Your part in this journey brings me both sadness and joy. Yet, you also spoke this book into existence as the storm began to rage and it is so.

A special acknowledge to every member of the Promise Worship Campus in Dallas, Texas for your prayers, thoughtful hugs, and fellowship. There were so many times your presence created an environment where wholeness became a possibility amongst scatter and broken pieces. To wholeness!

One never knows the final destination when the journey begins. I acknowledge the end of this journey came in part because of your touch upon my life.

Shalom to the Body of Christ without regard or respect of person, classification, or self-identification.

"But whoever denies me before men, I will also deny him

before My Father who is in heaven.

Matthew 10:33

Dedication

This collection of thoughts, mediations, and impartations from my heart is dedicated to my family and friends both immediate and extended, who have watched me throughout the years maturing from a lost child in to a fortified woman in and of God.

A special thanks to my mother who saw her child come through the fire and sometimes had the fire thrown in her direction and yet her unconditional love never changed its course from my direction. There is no greater love than that of a mother, you lived it, I felt it, and thank God, you believed! I love you.

A special thanks to Angel, my best friend and partner of eleven years who helped me to see what was missing in my life and what changes needed to be made to live out my voice. I wish the same level of understanding and purpose upon your life. Thank you immensely for never giving up on me, your solidarity during some very rough times means more to me than words could ever express. I love you for being you and allowing me to be me.

A special thanks to Pastor Alex D. Byrd of Living Faith Covenant Church, The Fellowship who carried me at times during the storm that engulfed my life, my mind, my heart, and my very identity. Even now the trueness of this statement demands pause for the reverence of living a life were your faith is your testimony and not your words along. Thank you for being a great man of God and role model to walk by in faith.

A special thanks to Elder Deneen Robinson who provided me a safe place to develop the skills necessary to have the courage to be so transparent about what was going on in my life as the storm raged on throughout the year. I emulated you until I could find me. Thank you for the hard lessons of cutting the umbilical of old habits and bad remixes. I consider you a friend who allowed me to figure out what the word meant in the context of faithfulness.

A special thanks to my surrogate Dad, Elder Marvin Roberts who in his quietness gave me a voice that had been screaming for release. I love you papa for opening up your home when I could not find one I felt safe in at the time. I pray this is just the beginning of great things to come for each of us.

A special thanks to everyone who has added to the summation of who I am today. Each of you played a role in getting this book into fruition.

Learning to love God above all else is the greatest thing I have ever done. I pray this book opens doors for others on or headed towards the same journey.

With the Love of Christ,

Dawn, Equally Yoked Heavenly Creation Services Inspired Word of God

Contents Page

1. Foreword .... Page xvii

2. Prologue .... Page 1

3. But God .... Page 9

4. Get Lost .... Page 14

5. If You Only Knew .... Page 19

6. Before .... Page 30

7. The Storm .... Page 37

8. Have You Ever Had an Experience with God .... Page 40

9. In God's Hand .... Page 49

10. Who Am I .... Page 63

11. Redemption .... Page 82

12. How on Earth Did This Happen? .... Page 93

13. Living Life on God's Terms .... Page 131

14. If You Conform to Anything, You Will Fall for Everything .... Page 144

15. Not Yet .... Page 151

16. I Stopped and Wondered .... Page 158

17. New Leader .... Page 172

18. Relationships .... Page 179

19. Journeys .... Page 183

20. Epilogue .... Page 190

21. About the Author's Year With God .... Page 194

Then the Lord said to Moses, "I will rain down bread from heaven for you. The people are to go out each day and gather enough for that day. In this way I will test them and see whether they will follow my instructions." Exodus 16:4 - 5

This page is intentionally left blank.

This page is intentionally left blank.

Foreword

There is a personal confession requiring a shedding of the light on having a conversation with the Great I AM. This year began with a deeply rooted call for change in my life. Often times over the years one will hear a word as a whisper and discount its relevance as applicable to their personal journey. He or she continues on as if the word had fallen on brittle land. A bird will come along and snap it up moving to greener pastures.

This book is the fruit of those greener pastures. The first day I sat down to write all the imagery within my vision, the Spirit responded and I submitted humbly unto its creative authority.

It began as a therapeutic outlet for some brokenness going on in the midst of my journey. As time allowed for a body of art to form, I recognized this truth: For out of the abundance of the heart, thy mouth shall speak.

The Spirit of the Loving God has spoken and here forth are personal words to me. I send forth the blessing of living water for the reader of this introspective reflection. Shalom.

If anyone would come after me, he must deny himself and take up his cross daily and follow me. For whoever wants to save his life will lose it, but whoever loses his life for me will save it. What good is it for a man to gain the whole world, and yet lose or forfeit his very self? If anyone is ashamed of me and my words, the Son of Man will be ashamed of him when he comes in his glory and in the glory of the Father and of the holy angels." Luke 9:23-26

Prologue

I was born Dawn Nichelle Boyland, a beautiful bouncing baby girl to my parents. Unfortunately or prophetically I exhibited several medical challenges to the doctors and nurses of St. Paul Hospital in Dallas, Texas at the time of my birth. Diagnosed with jaundice upon entry and a broken arm I spent approximately six weeks in the hospital in an incubator while the hands of God guided the minds of the doctors. It would appear I was just as stubborn, opinionated, and determined then as I am now. I must confess my truth even if I have difficulties with the journey to its source. God created me and then he spent most of my life modeling me into his likeness.

I had a normal childhood as any other southern born African American child in Texas. I grew up in a middle class family even though it would be many years before I realized the blessings upon my household in the southern sector of Dallas. God provided for all my needs, and I had many. He provided for most of my wants and I had even more of them then of the needs, but God provided for them all.

If the church doors opened on Sunday it was compulsory for me to be in attendance, bright-eyed, chirp, obedient, bible in tow, and my grandmother by my side. My mother would make sure I was ready by 7:00 a.m. every Sunday as she sent me out the door to hear the good news taught and preached by a Church of Christ Sunday school teacher and Church of Christ Pastor, respectively. There is an entire story on this one formative process of my life, which this book is not meant to relay, but provides some insight into the treasures of my heart. I attended vacation bible study every year faithfully. I loved the time spent learning about my heavenly Father even if I disagreed with the doctrine or teachings as displayed through human filters. I still relished in his presence before I knew it was the Holy Spirit guiding me into true awareness.

I recall many summer days of spiritual and theological debates between the neighborhood children, mostly my next door neighbor (play cousin, Lamont) as early as six or seven. We would have serious conversations about the truth of the gospel, the inconsistencies of the doctrines, and the reality of this truth, which neither of us really knew enough about we thought to dissuade the teachers of their source. Yet, it was a joyous time to fellowship in an uncanny way as a child, then and now. Baptized at nine I lived for Christ when it was most convenient and me the rest of the time, like most of my peers. The difference is I was overly moralistic and materialistic at the same time.

I remember being altruistic in nature during this time and most of my life. Many people, especially older generations often labeled me as being an "old spirit". Looking back at my life during this time the master weaved it all in an intrinsic manner. Its' ultimate unraveling so God could change the composition stored within, by confirming and reaffirming my beliefs rooted in his doctrine' and not man's scripted redaction according to man's agenda. At the very least I was old fashion. My dress, my attitude, my disposition about life and people were closer to my grandmother's than my peers.

I knew I was special, because I felt it when I spoke to God. My mother often reminded me I could be whatever I put my mind too, if I was willing to work harder than anyone else, including, and especially, "the white man". Sad, but true, this is after all the south. Closing one's eyes does not remove the sheets it only exacerbates the need for true cleansing. Here I have learned those of a darker skin are often considered unintelligent until proven otherwise. I proved it often. I prove it still.

Yet, I see no color or separation and I pray you see the same. I am a child of God. I see everyone whether they identify as Christian or not, as a child of God, as well. I confess and many would agree some of us make this declaration and revelation harder to receive of others, but press on I will. By now, it is assured, I enjoy the challenge. My life is a challenge in which the war has been won, but the battle scars although God's ended up on my personhood. He healed me, but first he sealed me from the storm of 2010. A storm touching everyone I know in one way or another.

The year two thousand ten began with many promises for a joyous year. I saw visions of great prosperity and much personal success. I felt as if I could conquer the world and anything it threw my way. This year proved it to be true. I realized what God foretells and how you get to it are not always clear in the moment. Sometimes he reveals you a benchmark of future achievements, but leads you down a valley of present disappointments. I take the liberty in making to the reader of this book this personal perspective and assessment of a journey foreseen, but never expected. Yet, for each disappoint I cleared the objective of the lesson. There were many times were my appointed and ordained angels felt the lesson needed repeating. So, repeat I did. I have confirmed herein how much I despise repetition beyond any semblance of enjoyment within any realm of possible goal attainment. I wish others held such a belief. Yet, with each obstacle course of my life for 2010 I grew stronger in spiritual recognition and dedication to the Great I Am.

I began this book as some outlet to speak forth all the confusion of my circumstances, which engulfed me in the New Year. As God began to speak, my body and mind were not ready for the lesson or the blessings I had spent many years praying for on so many nights. I wanted to hear God's voice, audibly. During the first week of January things began happening to me, which have forever changed how I view the spirit world and its ability to create and destroy.

My life story of this transformation and spiritual lesson in the balance between truth, fiction, and reality is currently in process through the working title, *The Journals – My Conversations with God.* There is no future date for publication at this time as I am chronicling the journey until God says it is time to display the process to his masterpiece at work.

I can however provide the reader of this book with this insight into the journey still unfolding, which I am still transcribing. I am different in many respects from the shell I was in the beginning of this year. The Great I Am has transformed me into something greater than I ever thought I would become. I am a magnificent vessel set apart for his use to assist in bringing awareness to the importance of holding on to your faith in the midst of the storm. This book chronicles the rough seas of the storm of 2010 while offering a believer a map, a light, a choice, and a hope for the rainbow of survival; if she or he can just hold on to the storm master. I did and this is a compilation of poetry and prose regarding and discussing the inward journey I traveled.

Jesus answered, "You would have no power over me, if it were not given to you from above. Therefore the one who handed me over to you is guilty of a greater sin."

John 19:11

But God

January 6, 2010

Sometimes to find yourself you have to lose yourself, because it is in the losing that you learn the value of what matters the most... God, Family, and Love, and for me it requires that it be in that order. Of course, there is an understanding that God and Love are truly one in the same.

Live long enough and God will change you if you allow it. Unfortunately, too often many of us, myself included battle with God even to our own detriment. I confess over the years when I dwell in things that are not meant for me I am capable of forgetting my charge, because I get loss, **BUT GOD!**

So in this New Year as I watch friends, family, and acquaintances alike make their New Year's Resolutions and promises to be made anew I **THANK GOD**, for he alone has brought me through and he alone will finish his good work within me. I am humbled to be an instrument in his great plan. I know there will be challenges I must face, battles that must be won, souls that require saving, and adversaries that will be working in concert to see that all of these matters defeat me, **BUT GOD!**

Every challenge, every battle, every seemly victory by the enemy for the souls' of God's children, and every adversary has already been defeat declares the **LORD**, and I cherish that promise as I claim what has been rightfully given unto me.

The governing **Truth** walking in love means never having to say you are sorry, because God went before is the key to personal liberation, relationship harmony, and spiritual maturity.

You see I have learned when God goes before...the conversation, the message, the thought, the verbalization, the plan, or the actions then the provisions for successes are already in place.

I just need to claim it, own it, and **PRAISE GOD** for the revelation and security in knowing this...

I am a child of God.

I have been given a strict charge in this life that can only be accomplished according to God's will aligned by his hand.

I need not worry about my problems, because...

My God is bigger than all my problems and if I remain focus on him,

I come to the understanding my problems are mere pebbles in comparison to the covering and provision of the Almighty.

Pebbles may hurt; they may even draw blood, **BUT GOD!**

So in this time and this place the definition of SELF is

discerned for me and all who receive it as:

Saving

Everything

Lasting

Forever

And, only **I AM** and those things belonging to the **Great I AM** fall

within this definition.

So to all with the ears to hear, eyes to see, hearts and minds to

discern... as the New Year reigns on you, set remembrance

towards this key of the kingdom: no matter what trials and

tribulations abound,

BUT GOD!

This page is intentionally left blank.

Get Lost

January 7, 2010

Get Lost... I dare you.

Get lost in God sometimes and see what happens as he shows you the way out to a bigger, brighter, and better way of life. A new life with Jesus as your source and foundation providing sustainable living water rooted in purpose and provision, God's household receives.

We spend so much time getting lost in things that have nothing to do with us. For these are things have the potential to change the course of our lives forever and most often they do, because we are *so focused on*:

Someone else's life,

Someone else's death,

Someone else's abundance,

Someone else's lack,

Someone else's choice,

Someone else's opinion,

Someone else's plans,

Someone else's actions,

Someone else's passiveness,

Someone else's aggressiveness,

Someone else's masculinity,

Someone else's femininity,

Someone else's pain,

Someone else's pleasure,

Someone else's hope,

Someone else's despair,

Someone else's job,

Someone else's leisure,

Someone else's blessings,

Someone else's curses,

Someone else's problem,

Someone else's solution,

Someone else's love,

Someone else's hate,

Someone else's victory,

Someone else's defeat,

Someone else's joy,

Someone else's power,

Someone else's authority,

Someone else's mate,

Someone else's singleness,

Someone else's desires,

Someone else's dream,

Someone else's nightmare,

Someone else's peace,

Someone else's turmoil,

Someone else's story,

Someone else's nevertheless…*when what we really need is to get lost in SELF!*

And not the SELF of the natural, but of the spiritual; a SELF that says I am saving everything lasting forever, by adhering to the **Truth** in the whispers of God!

Do you hear the whisper?

Can you feel his embrace?

Are you marvel ling at his glory?

Does his light shine down on you?

Were you surprised at his sweet caress the first time he spoke?

If the answer is no to any of these questions, than perhaps, like so many of his children you have forgotten the order of God's perfect plan...God First. For when God is first, everything becomes second, and all things become clear in his presence.

So today, I dare you...**GET LOST**.

This page is intentionally left blank.

If You Only Knew

January 8, 2010

If you only knew how I crafted you from scratch with love, authority, grace, and the plans I have in store for you.

Would you still focus on your current situation or press forward beyond your reality into my spirituality?

If you only knew that what you envision determines my response.

Would you still limit me by visualizing lack over abundance?

Or would you alter your vision?

If you only knew that the love I have for you is all consuming and all knowing.

Would you still lie about the intentions of your heart?

If you only knew that your heart determines your actions.

Would you still feed it doubt, confusion, despair, hate, un-forgiveness, and things designed to bring forth death and not life?

Or would you stop to sow the spirit of faith, clarity, hope, love, mercy, and things that speak of life?

If you only knew that the power to change your situation cannot be found in a bottle or pill, but in the well of Living Water.

Would you drink? Would you share it with those less fortunate

than you?

If you only knew that your neighbor's blessings depended on your response to the call.

Would you care? Would you respond?

Or, would you turn and walk away saving God's

blessing for a later day when his Angel stood before

you.

If you only knew that the authority I have provided to you in my name is the most powerful tool you possess.

Would you use it?

Or would you overlook the treasures in your war chest, because the package was different than expected.

If you only knew the hurdles you have already defeated, the victories you have already won, the life you have already lived, the people you have already touch, the saints you have already met, the love you have already given and received, the life you have already saved, the dream you have already made come true, the time you have already redeemed, the angels you have entertained, the party I have prepared in your honor on that good and faithful day.

Would it change you?

Or would you stay the same living in poverty when I have prepared you a place of wealth and a feast fit for royalty?

If you only knew that I have outlined specific promises of

scientific proportions about how you press forward and through.

Would you use them?

Or would you deliver your inheritance over to the

enemy of your progression without even a call to the

avenger of salvation, glory, and honor.

If you only knew that every promise I have only works when you

hide it within your heart.

Would you?

Or, decide to take the road less traveled and receive the

brokenness of lost without purpose.

If you only knew that unlike the promises of men my promises are

eternal without regard or respect of person.

Would you challenge me?

Or would the challenges over take you because you decided to believe in the promises of the temporal over the promises of the eternal?

If you only knew that you can ask me anything and if you believe it has been received in the spirit I have indwelt in you - it is yours.

Would you ask?

Or, have you forgotten how to call me.

I tell you now, I tell you later, and I tell you always that if you knew what I knew you would look into the mirror and see life abundantly.

You would see hope in a hopeless situation.

You would see light in the dead of night.

You would see peace in the midst of the storm, if you even saw the storm.

You would see what I see when I look at you…**ME!**

So as you go through this day…

Start by changing your sight.

Began to seek me;

Began to romance me;

Began to know the One that first knew you;

Began to ask me what you need;

Began to question your thoughts;

Began to pattern your actions;

Began to connect with others whom speak life to your situations;

Began to inspire the uninspired;

Began to claim the plans I have for you, the love I have given you;

Began to relish in my presence;

Began to live the life you were created to live.

For it is in the beginning and through the initiation of the process that the transition takes creates an environment for transformation.

If you remember nothing, remember that in order to begin the journey you must first accept the charge and all that comes with it.

That sometimes living means dying and dying means living. I can give you life, but what you do with it relies on you.

I loved you when I made you.

I love you when you fell.

I love you when you left me.

I will love you when you decide to return.

For you are bone of my bone, flesh of my flesh, and spirit of my spirit.

Claim me and enjoy the journey.

For if you only knew...

"And everyone who calls on the name of the Lord will be saved; for on Mount Zion and in Jerusalem there will be

deliverance as the Lord has said, among the survivors

whom the Lord calls." Joel 2:32

But whatever I am now, it is all because God poured out

his special favor on me—and not without results. For I

have worked harder than any of the other apostles; yet

it was not I but God who was working through me by his

grace. 1 Corinthians 15:10

This page is intentionally left blank.

Before

January 9, 2010 and January 28, 2010

Before there was an earth to walk upon,

I loved you.

And now you love me.

Before there was air to breathe,

I supplied you with lungs to exhale releasing my synergy,

And words to change the world while creating new ones in

spiritual energy.

Before you knew me,

I desired to know you.

And now we do.

Before there was you,

There was me at the head of the tree.

And you are the closest branch to my heart.

For I am what you seek even though the mystery has yet to be

revealed,

> You feel me.

> And I feel you too.

Before hot fudge and ice cream,

> We made the perfect couple…

> You learning to walk in your authority

> And me gleaming with joy

Before there was bacon and eggs,

> We made the perfect couple…

> You sitting in my lap listening to the sweet, sweet whispers

of my voice

And me filling your heart with joy

Before there was Heaven and Hell,

We made the perfect couple...

You basking in my light

And me warmed by your response

Before there was mother and child,

We made the perfect couple...

You secure with me in your heart

And me guarding you until you could speak what had been

written there in my secret dwelling place.

For I am what you seek even though the mystery has yet to be
revealed,

You feel me.

And I feel you too.

Before there was turmoil and mistrust,

I was there for you

And you were waiting for me.

Before there was doubt and confusion

I was your way out of darkness

And you were on the right path and my inner light

projected outwardly through you.

Before there was a disconnection and need for reflection

I was your connection

And you were able to feel my affection

Before there was a need to heal and recover

I was your solution

And you were my conclusion

For I am what you seek even though the mystery has yet to be revealed,

You feel me.

And I feel you too.

As I was on the road, approaching Damascus about noon,

a very bright light from heaven suddenly shone down

around me. Acts 22:6

Immediately, Jesus said, "Calm down! It's me. Don't be

afraid!" Matthew 14:27

The Storm

January 14, 2010

Sometimes you need a storm.

A storm has amazing cleansing power for the soul, the mind, and the body. It can wash away the dirt that has collected unnoticed by its inhabitants. It has the ability to create debris requiring a closer inspection of what is trash and treasured. We often get confused about the two, but deep reflections allows for clarity of the matter at hand. So today, I praise God for the storm, because there is always sunshine after the rain. A rainbow comes to remind us of the creator's promise.

A new day is born and old ways, habits, and barriers are washed away. Have you had your storm? Are you weighed down by debris? Are you confused? It is ok; many of us become confused during the storm. It is in these times that we need to hold on to the storm master. He may not have authored your storm, but rest in the knowledge of his supreme navigation ability through the rough seas before you. Everything has value to the storm master even your fear of the waves, because your fear is needed so the storm master can inspect them and rout out any unhealthy fear preventing you from overcoming the storm.

There is a difference between healthy and unhealthy fear. Healthy fear tells us that sometimes it is not wise for us to handle the shark in the storm, but it is ok to remove the seaweed. Unhealthy fear prevents the storm master from navigating your storm, thus, perpetuating your experience in the storm beyond its appointed time. Have you met the storm master? Can I guide you through your first introduction, if not? *I acknowledge the Christ within me, I recognize this life, death, and resurrection, and I give him complete and total authority over my life.* For it is assured he wants to train you, but first you must release the anchor holding you back from receiving his instruction.

If you are in the midst of the storm, stop fighting the waves and flow with them. There is treasure to be found, but only a free saint can receive it. Strive to be free by becoming a slave. It was hard to learn being a slave was not a bad thing if you were a slave to the right thing. What are you a slave too? Your answer will navigate you to either captivity or freedom. My choice may not by your choice, but a choice is required. You can make the choice or allow someone to make the choice for you. Either way, welcome to the storm.

Choose to bring along the only undefeated captain of the sea of life and death.

Have You Ever Had an Experience with God?

February 12, 2010

Have you ever had an experience with God?

I mean a real experience. A type of experience in which God takes your world, turns it upside down, inside out, and back around again. This type of experience has much value. It cleanses the spirit, soothes the soul, and revitalizes the body. Nevertheless, it is not a one-time event. It must occur daily, sometimes, hourly, minute-by-minute, or second-by-second. It must be an on-going journey. One where new treasures are discovered each day, reflected on, and then practiced in your daily walk upon the earth.

It is through an experience with God your life takes on true meaning. God has predesigned events focused on placing your life's journey on the big screen for all to see who are connected to you in the great circle of life. It occurs this way, because it is not until a public review of your life's experiences, decisions, and consequences are examined that you introspective view is fully complete. We often fail to see what is right in front of us, because we have failed to have the experience. Some have it daily and therefore do not require much reflection, because they are actively living the experience out. However, there are others like myself who fear the experience.

Many have their own reason for why they fear the experience, but I think for me in this moment the fear comes from the perceived consequences real, mentally or spiritually created. Yet, sometimes consequences have their own peace of treasure. Consequences let you know what is right, what is not, and what needs changing. There have been many consequences in my life for failing to have the experience. Some may never be rectified, others have already begun to heal, but it is through the experience you find out what has been given to you, what has been given to others, and what God has given to no one.

You also learn there is not much given to you if it is not about you in the first place or connected to the covenant you have made with and through God. We need to consider changing lanes when we find ourselves working or seeking things strictly ordained for anybody, but us. Each of us has a purpose in life and having learned its meaning in my life gives me hope even in the midst of the storms. There are some who know what their purpose or calling as God ordained it to be long before heaven and earth existed. Others are just beginning to learn what their purpose is and some know, but choose not to walk in it. I confess I am not quite sure what my purpose is, like so many others I suspect, but at least I recognize that I have a purpose to fulfill. It is up to me to let go, let God, and be willing to accept the charge no matter what it is or what I may need to do to achieve it. It is the reminder to get lost for SELF.

When you have an experience with God, he does a Great and Amazing thing. He brings you into a personal awareness, which never existed before. He pushes us through and sometimes he has to carry us, because we have loss the strength to carry ourselves, but carry us he does, until we can carry ourselves. Lest we forget that he can carry us when we cannot carry ourselves we run the risk of becoming lost again, so be mindful of the journey, the potholes, and traps of the enemy, for they will surely come, BUT GOD.

You see I have come to a new awareness that God is God and no one, but God can do the work God has set out to do in you. I cannot help him, because I only delay what he has in store. Are you trying to help God out on the plans he has for you? If so, why, because he is the designer and creator so he has the plans all worked out well in advance of your entry into the earth. If he needed your help then how could you call on him when you needed him the most? You could not, because you would lack the faith to believe he could do what he has promised to do. More importantly what he surely will do, if you believe, and have the faith with a whole measure of trust in him that he will do exactly what he said he would do. A God promise is a certified check for a future blessing.

Therefore, I asked the question again. Have you had your experience with God? If not, try it out sometimes and see the journey he takes you on. Sometimes it will not be pretty. Sometimes you may just want to call out and say I quit, enough is enough and I cannot take any more, sometimes you might even quit – *for a while and hopefully not for a long spell for your sake*, but if you keep pressing then God is able, willing, and can do exactly what he promised. Trust and believe what has already been done, because you simply do not have the eyes to see yet, but ask God and he will never lead you astray. Because sometimes if God showed us the path required for attainment of our inheritance we would run in the opposite direction never coming through to the other side. To a place far better than where we started the journey.

Now, there is another part to this. You must know what God said he is able, willing, and would do. These aspects of God can only be discovered in conjunction with reading his word, and listening to his voice. A voice only meant for you to hear through personal reflection and self-inventory. Now at some point you may be asked to share what you have learned for the benefit of others, but hold on to God for that time, because only he knows when the fruit is ready for picking. Some fruit may appear ready, but has not met its due season while other fruit may become ripe if you fail to pick it in its due season, so only God knows when the time is or should be, even if you are the one to do the picking. Some call it a harvest, but I proclaim the feast after the harvest.

In concerning self-inventory, be mindful it requires work – and a big warning to the wise it often calls for great sacrifice and hard work, which comes with a lot of pain. The realization of what your outward self truly represented instead of what you thought it represented is a catalyst for the experience. However, do not lose face or faith, because if you had never done the work and continue to do the work you would never know what did not align with God whom can only work with what aligns with him and in him. Are you connected with God? Or, do you simply need a realignment, which happens sometimes if we stop doing the work. This in and of itself says we should always be focused on the work and not the fruit of the journey, for fruit comes from God's design and is his responsibility to reveal as he decrees.

Each of us has a responsibility to one another and some of us choose to overlook that responsibility while others jump in all feet in only to find out they have jumped into the wrong pot. Nevertheless, even if you should happen to jump into the wrong pot it still has value. God is able to bring you out and place you where you can do his work as he meant you to accomplish it. Prayerfully, the next time you will wait on God to place you where he wants you instead of where you *think* he wants you to be, because many times they are not the same pot or may not be ready to receive what you have been sent to give freely and with a cheerful heart.

If you have never had your experience with God or it has been awhile then I would say today is a good day as any to have an experience that only God can give and bring you through! The experience is not the key, but treasure source of you, me, and the true deity both in heaven and on earth.

This page is intentionally left blank.

In God's Hands

February 14, 2010

How do you know when you are resting in God hands?

I never quite understood at my core what people in the church meant when they would say just put it in God's hand and he will take care of it. Here is a better one for you, "Lay it at the altar, and God will take it from there." What do you mean by put it in God's hand or lay it at the altar, I would think to myself and sometimes I might even say it aloud? How can I take this tangible object or intangible feeling, issue, problem, matter, whatever and place it into God's hand to handle for me. It belongs to me and thus I must be the one to resolve it. Yet, what really belongs to us? When we get down to the heart of the matter God provides the very breath we breathe to each of us. We have no control in the action. We cannot alter his decision, sometimes. We are not powerful enough to convince him not to change his mind if he sees fit to progress in a certain direction. We do not even get a say in the matter of how fast or slow he breaths. If he decided not to breathe life into you or me, we would simply fade from this earth without as much as a tear.

Yet, God does care for us even in our sinfulness, separation, desperation, loneness, sadness, pain, trials, or simply our lack. We all lack something that only God can feel and fulfill, but many are unaware of what that lack is and this mastery has the potential to destroy our souls if we are not connected to the one that provides all. There is a reason one of God's name is Jehovah Jireh. That reason can be found in the truth God provides all we could every dream about or hope to have. For those who are not aware Jehovah Jireh translates to "God provides." We would also be mindful to remember everything we have or ever will have comes from him and through him. That is why Jesus said, "Because you know me, you know my Father!" What greater father could any of us have than the one who loved us so much he would forsake himself so that we might be saved, so we could receive his salvation?

Salvation comes in many forms. Sometimes it is just the idea you are not alone and there is someone bigger and greater than you could ever hope to be. Sometimes it comes in the midnight sorry creeping in as night begins to turn to day. Sometimes it happens as you grieve that lost love affair. Sometimes it comes when everything you valued is tarnished and you do not see a way of polishing up the ruminants. Sometimes it comes simply by stopping to hear his voice. Other times it is already there, but we fail to give way for it to work in our lives. Honestly, it is always there, but we are too focused on what is not there to see what is present. Remember the greatest gift God provides is his free-gift of salvation to those who will receive it as he gives it.

Being in God's hands means something different to different people and here is what it means to me.

Even when my situation says otherwise, I am loved by the Great I AM.

Even when it looks as if the war has been lost, I am loved by the Great I AM.

Even when all hope appears to be lost, I am loved by the Great I AM.

Even when I fail to live up to the character of God as he intends, I am loved by the Great I AM.

Even when the obstacles continue to mount and mount, I am loved by the Great I AM.

Even when the enemy would have me to believe that I have been defeated, I am loved by the Great I AM.

Even when I cannot make a way out of a way, I am loved by the Great I AM.

Even when everything that I loved has been taken away from me, I am loved by the Great I AM.

Even when joy has been lost, I am loved by the Great I AM.

Even when peace cannot be found no matter where I look, I am loved by the Great I AM.

Even when the story has ended, I am still loved by the Great I AM.

Even when the story has just begun, I am loved by the Great I AM.

Even when I cannot see, I am loved by the Great I AM.

Even when Mother Nature releases her fury that creates destruction, I am loved by the Great I AM.

Even when people leave me for being who God called me out of confusion to become, I am loved by the Great I AM.

Even when I should have lost my mind, because of what I have gone through, I am loved by the Great I AM.

Even when I did lose my mind for a spell, I am loved by the Great I AM.

Even when I lost my home, I am loved by the Great I AM.

Even when I lost my job, I am loved by the Great I AM.

Even when the future I had perfectly planned is gone astray, I am loved by the Great I AM.

Even when there was no way to turn, because I had turned every which way, but loose, I am loved by the Great I AM.

Even when I choose not to sacrifice my wants for the needs of others, I am loved by the Great I AM.

Even when my affections are not returned in the manner I see fit, I am loved by the Great I AM.

Even when I am demanding, condescending, and overbearing, I am still loved by the Great I AM.

Even when I am overwhelmed, I am loved by the Great I AM.

Even when I can go no more, I am loved by the

Great I AM.

Even when I choose not to perform, as I know God has ordained

me unto his purpose, I am loved by the

Great I AM.

Even when sorry reigns, I am loved by the Great I AM.

Even when the smile on the outside hides the frown on the inside, I

am loved by the Great I AM.

Even when truth is hard to find – no matter where I seek it, I am

loved by the Great I AM.

Even when the lie I tell is to myself, I am loved by the Great I AM.

Even when the treasures of my soul are wasted on the dead of this world, I am loved by the Great I AM.

Even when I have become a part of the deadly world, I am loved by the Great I AM.

Even when my integrity has been lost, I am loved by the Great I AM.

Even when enough is not enough, I am loved by the Great I AM.

Because,

God loved me before I knew how to love myself.

God loved me before I recognized what love was.

God loved me before I made a decision conscious or otherwise to go against him with my actions, yet he has an amazing power to redeem that, which belongs to him even if it was lost for a spell.

I was lost for a period. I am not quite sure when the period began or how it even started. I grew up in a loving home as any other I suppose. I have two loving parents whom loved me as best as they could regardless of my assessment of the fact. One remains on earth and the other now resides in heaven.

Moreover, my mother continues to show me the love of God after all I have put her through over the years.

When I thought I had nowhere to turn, I could turn to her for guidance, instruction, hope, love, and yes, peace. Peace is a mindset and now a particular place.

I never really treasured this gift before, because I took it for granted. When you lose everything you have measured by human standards, you start taking inventory and find out permanent losses were never yours to begin with. I lost myself and it has been a long arduous climb back to reality of how I am supposed to be. I confess I have not made it back completely, but I am willing to continue the journey, because I know it is all for my good and those willing to hear my testimony.

No one really knows what God is doing, but God. Sometimes he shares a little with each of us, and sometimes he does not. Yet, we have to continue to push even when it appears we have hit a brick wall. I know of no greater being than God who has a hammer to break down any wall, including the wall on the inside we hide even from ourselves.

In addition, be very mindful each of us has some form of a wall on the inside of which only God can breakdown, if we are willing. Are you willing to be broken for his good? Do you need to be broken for your God? Are you in the midst of your brokenness? Have you overcome the brokenness? Is the brokenness too consuming in your current state of mind? Whatever state of consciousness you may currently be in, trust in something I had to learn recently myself.

God loves you. God knows who you are even if you do not. God expects nothing more of you than he has provided you to give freely so others may have a need for what you have. God is greater than any problem you are facing in this moment. God knew about the problem and the deliverance before you even had the experience. He may have even orchestrated it for your benefit. God will never leave you in your darkest hour. God can do far more than you could ever imagine and will if you get out the way. God is love, and he gives that love to you without question, even if you choose not to receive it.

O' how great it is to be in God's hand. Even setbacks have no power over your destiny, and not because you are entitled to it in anyway, but because God needs your setbacks to get you back on track. Are you off track? I was and getting back will be a life-long journey. However, in this I rest...I am in God's hand now, forever, and always. Truthfully, I always have been. I just did not recognize it at times and nothing or no one has the power to change this truth. Praise God for where you are no matter what you are facing, because when things are placed in God's hand, it is already done!

God said to Moses, "I AM WHO I AM. This is what you are to say to the Israelites: 'I AM has sent me to you.'" Exodus 3:14

For he confirmed to me he is Alpha and Omega beyond the corners of my mind

Who am I?

May 8, 2010

Who am I is a question I believe everyone asks themselves at one time or another in their lives. Some of us ask the question often during our formative years as we attempt to navigate this thing called life.

Some of us ask the question as we work through all the pains of our past. Some of us ask the question as we drive ourselves to work. Some of us ask the question as we walk to school. Some of us ask the question as we sit in our bedrooms thinking about life in general. Some of us ask the question as we fail to recognize whom we could potentially be if we put the effort into being who we are not. Some of us ask the question as we sit with our parents in front of the television.

Some of us ask the question as we sit in the pew. Some of us ask the question as we play in the field. Some of us ask the question as we fight with our spouse or partner. Some of us ask the question as we prepare our meals. Some of us ask the question as we make love with our mate.

Some of us ask the question as we play with our children. Some of us ask the question as we listen to our friends talk about who they think they are. Some of us ask the question as they rise above the pack. Some of us ask the question as they fall below the masses.

Some of us ask the question as they learn to think for themselves. Some of them ask the question as others tell them who they think they are or should be. Some of us ask the question as we cut our lawns.

Some of us ask the question as we have lunch with a co-worker never really engaging in the conversation, because we are so focused on us rather, then on them. Some of us ask the question while we take our showers or dress our children. Some of us ask the question while we read our Bibles. Some of us ask the question while we participate in Bible Studies across the land.

Some of us ask the question while we sing our praises to the Lord, which some of us doubt even exists silently. Some of us ask the question while we pay our bills that never seem to end. Some of us ask the question while we contemplate our next action.

Some of us ask the question while we debate the truth of the need for the answer. Some of us ask the question while we decide if where we are is really, where we should be or simply where we have settled to exist. Some of us ask the question during a sermon.

Some of us ask the question as we walk across the stage to accept our degrees or diplomas depending on our current track. Some of us ask the question as we get our haircut and recognize that others around us appear to know themselves. Yet, we never question if this is a projection of our belief or a reality of fact.

Some of us ask the question as we lay in the hospital bed dying and wondering if we ever figured out the answer. Some of us ask the question as we attend a funeral and then wonder why we just decided to consider the question, now.

Some of us ask the question simply, because we believe it is a question worth asking even if we really do not want to know the answer. Some of us ask the question as a part of a school assignment only to recognize we should have asked the question well before now. Some of us ask the question, because not asking the question says more than to actually ask the question and not have an answer.

Some of us ask the question so we can say we have when it comes up in conversation. Yet, we never delve into the depths of the question, never leaving the surface level. Some of us ask the question because we are inquisitive and we like to ask questions, but never care to find out the answers.

Some of us ask the question, because it is a question many others have asked before. Some of us ask the question, because life almost demands we have asked the question. Some of us ask the question then ask it again, and again, and again. Yet we never seem to find an answer that is satisfactory to what we feel on the inside somewhere deep within. Some of us ask the question because it is a question by almost everyone we connect with, whether in a new relationship, a job interview, a class discussion, or a person on the street while we go throughout the mundane actions of our daily lives finding a place on our lips.

This question almost, always leads to another question, which is who am I not. Well, here is what I can tell you about me today. I am not a slave to my own desires. I am not a poverty-stricken black woman. I am not a liar by habit, I was at one point, but I am not today. I am not a theft.

I am not a lesbian, by design.

I hold the belief my God is no respecter of person. I believe when my God looks upon me he sees neither male nor female. I believe my God only sees Jesus when he looks upon me, which is how I strive daily to look upon the people I encounter. I believe this with all I am and all that is within me.

So when I make the statement that I am not a lesbian by design, it is not a condemnation, but a revelation, I am more than a title or a disposition. I am, because the one who live within me is, I AM. So, there is no confusion or attempt to claim I meant something I did not this is to clarify the Truth. My God created it all and made available the "free gift of grace" for all who confess with their mouth, and believe in their hearts, of the one true Messiah. I affirm this to be the governing foundation of my heart, my life, walk, and my testimony.

I believe my God has two primary focuses for a relationship. The first one being love and the second being commitment beyond these principles I believe my God does not care how we mate or if we mate as long as the relationship is full of love, commitment, and faithfulness to God and each other.

I am not a fool. I am not a demon or demon possessed. I am not a loser. I am not a gangster. I am not a failure. I am not a single-mother. I am not a convict. I am not a whore. I am not a cheater.

I am not a deceiver. I am not a rebel, by my father's definition - not mine and surely not the world's definition.

I am not a sinner. I am not a perfectionist even when my outward character would designate otherwise. I am not a two-timer. I am not anything that the world would like to affix to me.

I may have been all or none of these things before I met and fell in love with Christ. There may even be days where I forget who I am not and decide to return to who I use to be. Yet, this is not who my Father calls me. Nor will I answer to any of these labels.

Yes, I can be any of these on any given day and some days I just might be, because I forget who I am. I can be any of these, for many of us this is the only name we are comfortable living out. Yet, this is not who I am and this is not who you are.

When Christ came upon this Earth, he changed our names. He cleansed our spirit. He cleansed our hearts. He cleansed our minds. He cleansed our will. He cleansed all wrongness with the new status given to us a result of Adam. Yet, we refuse to accept what he did for us, because we continue to live as who we are not. The thing is if we accept Christ, then he no longer sees us as who we purport ourselves to be in the earth. He sees the blood of his sacrifice.

So why are so many of us bent on living out a life not meant to be our lives. Our situation is similar to a millionaire's son leaving home and going to live as a homeless man. He lives on the street. He looks for food in the trash. He cannot find shelter from the storms raging throughout the night. He cannot seem to recognize he has a home waiting for him, if only he would return.

He questions his very existence. He questions why his family has turned their back on him. Yet, he never comes to the truth, which is he turned his back on his family and not his family on him. He goes day after day falling deeper into depression, because no one loves him or so his perception believes this to be true. He falls between the cracks.

He loses all hope. He finally decides to take his life, because no one would care anyway. He decides to make it quick. He finds the tallest bridge and writes the letter. He walks to the bridge thinking about how his life has become so meaningless. He prepares to say goodbye to the world that gave up on him when he was at his zenith. As he prepares to end what is no longer a great life in his eyes, his father happens to be driving on this bridge the same time he is about to jump. A life I might add that is not his life to end. His father sees the son he loves. The son he has been missing since the day he abruptly left home so long ago. His father at first does not even believe his eyes.

Could this be true? Could this be his son whom left home so long ago, ready to conquer the world on his own? Could this be his son he has spent many sleepless nights thinking about how he was or what he was doing? Could this be his son? Could there be a possibility the son he thought died long ago was actually standing before him about to take his own life? Could it be?

Could the son he was so sure needed no one reached the point where he was ready to seek help from anyone? Could it be?

Could it be a figment of his imagination? Could it be even possible that his son he birthed, cared for all those years, raised up to be more than he had become, taught him how to follow his heart, and schooled him on the traps of life had reached such a low point in his life. Could it be?

He approaches his son at first confused on whether or not it was indeed his son or if he simply hopes it might be, because they have not communicated in so long, they no longer knew each other.

He taps him on the back making sure not to startle him. His son does not respond.

He pulls on his jacket. His son does not respond.

He pulls on his hand. His son does not respond. His son does not respond.

He calls his name. His son does not respond.

He hugs him from behind. His son does not respond.

He picks up a rock and throws it at him and it draws blood. His son does not respond.

He finds a large stick and hits him over the head. His son does not respond.

He goes to his car and gets a lighter. He uses the lighter to set his son's coat on fire.

His son moves, but does not respond.

He puts the fire out. He gets a tire iron from his car and whacks his son in the back. His son moves again, but other than that makes no further movement.

He goes and gets two friends to help move his son from the ledge. His son moves, but does not respond.

He takes his son home and feeds him. His son eyes open, but other than that he makes no movement. He washes his son. Yet, his son makes no further movement. He gives his son a haircut. His son stands up, but does not speak.

He takes his son to the movie of his son's life. His son starts to watch it, but does not make much movement. The movie continues to play and play until it comes to the point where the son made the conscious decision to leave his Father's home and go his own way. The son rewinds the movie. The son begins to make noises.

The son is now actively watching his life on the big screen. The son notices some things he had forgotten. His parents loved him. His parents feed him. His parents cared for him when he could not care for himself. His parents taught him how to be a man.

His parents watched him grow up and always provided for his needs. His parents did not leave him. He left his parents. They stand up. He looks at his father. He cries. He cries some more. He cries even more. He weeps. He cries. He falls to his knees. He falls to his father's feet. He cries and clings to his father leg. He begins to weep and praise his father for always being there even when he could not see it. He asks for forgiveness, which his father gave long before he asked. He receives it. They leave the movie. The next chapter of his life begins.

Now, this son recognizes that he has far more than he realized. He after all is a millionaire's kid living in poverty. He is after all, the child of an esteemed man. He is royalty. He is more than he became. He can be anything he wants to be and his dad is right there to make sure he is everything he is supposed to be. Why did he miss this the first time around you might ask? He does. He comes to the understanding that he had it so easy before that he never appreciated what he had until he lost it all. He knows better now. The trees are bigger. The grass is greener. The clouds are fluffier. The people are nicer. Things appear to be so much better than it was before or is it. His father tells him something many us are blessed enough to know without doing it alone already know or come to know without leaving home – his situation has not changed. The trials and tribulations he had out there on his own have forever shaped his perception of how he views his past, present, and future. It was always good. It was always peaceful. He had love back then. Going it alone forced him to re-prioritize his focus. He reaches another conclusion for he will never go it alone again.

So as it was said in one of my favorite movies: "It's the question that drives us, but what we really want to know is the answer!" Why is not so important as how. How do I change what I cannot see? How do I alter my lack of self- confidence? How do I overcome the impossible? How do I, correct my past mistakes? How I do I find the truth? How do I rectify the lies? How do I correct the shortcomings within myself? How do I come to the understanding that I cannot do any of it on my own? How do I let go of everything that holds me from finding the answer? How do I accomplish what I cannot understand? How do I make it work for my good? How do I rise above it all? How do I find my identity, which I lost so long ago I no longer remember what it is? How do I return to my father's mansion?

I die. I fall on my knees. I pray to my father. I pray he changes my will to his. I pray he changes my heart to his. I pray he changes my thoughts to his. I pray he changes my speech to his. I pray he changes my actions to his. I request he remove everything he has not placed within me from me. I ask his forgiveness for leaving our home. I give myself permission to become close to him again as we once were. I make another request for the removal of all things unlike him of which I cannot see or holds no value to your purpose in your life in this vessel. I ask that he search me. I ask that he heal me. I ask that he enter me. I give him unrestricted permission to fill me. I hold nothing back. I completely free myself to become someone completely different in him. I let go of the fear. I let go of the doubt. I let go of myself. I die. I do what no one else, but I can do. I give myself the freedom to say that I can no longer live the life I am living and then I say to daddy he can come in and reorganize me from the inside out. He does.

I do not see it at first. I do not recognize the change. I notice that I speak differently. I notice that I think differently. I notice I act differently. I notice I am not who I use to be. I notice I actually function differently. I notice so much I recognize something else, which is this, he has transformed me, and I am no longer who I used to be, and I will never be the child of innocence again. He ensures it by the touch he gives me in this moment it is for my strengthening and not my harm. I trust him. I hold on to him. I live for him by his steady hands. I am my father's child.

Who I am, is not as important as who I should be in my Father.

What is your question that drives you?

Let your conversation be without love of money, satisfied

with your present circumstances; for he has said, I will

not leave thee, neither will I forsake thee.

Hebrews 13:5

All this is from God, who reconciled us to himself

through Christ and gave us the ministry of

reconciliation: 2 Corinthians 5:18

Redemption

May 19, 2010

There are things in life often taking one by surprise and you never truly understand what they are or why they exist until after the fact. There are things happening in your life, which causes you to take pause and reconcile what you see with what you believe. There are things happening in your life requiring a deeper inspection of truth from fiction. There are things happening in your life, which are incapable of being conceal in the moment, because in the moment you must be reactive instead of proactive. There are things testing every level of patience in an inpatient world. There are things requiring you to suffer through rejection, disappoint, lost, defeat, and persecution at the hands of those most close to you. Yet, it is a great reward to come to a comprehension nothing done in the presence of God and for the cause of God goes unrewarded.

There are things in this life I simply do not understand. There are things in this life I simply cannot explain away. There are things in this life no matter how hard I attempt to resolve the mystery the mystery remains. There are things cloaked for a season and then there are things revealed in their due season. All things have a time, a place, a purpose, a reason, a season, and an end. Yet, the clock is not ours, but God's. How great is it to know I have no power or control over the timing of the seasons to abound each day. It is a humbling feeling. It is a sobering feeling. It is a freeing feeling. It is a justified feeling. It is a feeling surpassing all understanding. It is a God's feeling.

Redemption comes in many forms. Redemption says God purified me of all the wrong within me. Redemption states without remorse all things done in the dark are now in the light. It just takes some

of us a minute to readjust our eyes because we have lived in darkness so long we do not recognize the switch turning on the light. Redemption says no one is safe unless darkness attains captivity. Redemption says if darkness reigns on then light becomes static and without power and the very definition of light is powerful. Some will have to suffer in order for the sanctification lost in darkness that has fused with the light. There is no remorse for saving a brother's soul even if he must lose his life in the process, for his life is temporal, but his soul is eternal. Redemption states corruption is no more. Redemption states that if one falls then until purification takes place we all have fallen.

Redemption states I am my brother's keeper and there are times where in order to keep my brother I may have to temporary cause him pain. It is a simple truism of life in the great circle of life. Causing pain is one of the most difficult things we may face in this life, in order to bring healing; yet, it is a necessary path towards wholeness. It is a service many of us would prefer never to have to perform.

Yet, I would hate to be before the father on that day and have to answer for my failures resulting in my standing alone before him instead of beside my brother. I would hate to be that person. I would fear being labeled such a saint. I would not want to risks such disregard for my spiritual brother upon my head. I would not and I shall not.

Therefore, it is of great pain and anguish that the light begins to shine. It is with a heavy heart that the switch has been set to turn on. Just as in the Lord, we do not know the time. We do not know the hour. We do not know the location. We do not know how, so we should be ready at any time for all things done in the dark are soon revealed by the light within me.

It is always calm before the storm. There is an eerie peace, which settles upon the land right before a major storm begins to form. I have felt it. I felt it particularly around February 7, 2010, and it was humbling. It is as if nature is preparing herself for the raging winds. It is as if nature is preparing herself for the rapid rains. It is as if nature can hear the tornados forming out in the distance and so she bears down for the storm ahead. **Bear down**. Bear down and tie you anchors to the nearest shoreline.

Bear down. Bear down and pray to God Almighty as you have never prayed before. Bear down.

Bear down and hold on tightly to your love ones; they will need this peace to sustain themselves through the storm ahead.

Bear down. ***Bear down.*** *Bear down.*

Most people make the mistake of not preparing for storms. The weather person comes on with a major announcement storms chasers have spotted storms in your immediate area. They say prepare your cabinets and stockpile your shelves for you will need them through the storm. They say board up your windows and hold your children close. They tell you so many things about safety and precautionary measures to keep you and yours safe. We do not listen. We believe our knowledge is superior to the one above forecast all or so we think. We leave our doors unprotected. We leave our children out in the yard. We do not fill the cabinets or stockpile our shelves. We do not pray.

The storm comes. The rain falls. The wind blows through the atmosphere. The surf rises. The tornados spin and destruction is thleir goal and they succeed on every account. This has to be the storm of the century. It is.

Hold on, because this storm will be a storm they will write about in every newspaper. This is a storm books upon books will be

written. From this storm movies are about to give birth. This storm will be what not to do before a storm happens. This will be the storm that teaches apprentice storm masters how to weather the storm. This storm will change the course of history as it has never been or will ever be again.

This storm is the one your mother warned about when you were just beginning to discern who you are within the earth. This is a storm and it will be mighty. Wow, this storm will redefine the integrity of our nation. This storm will take the land of the free and the home of the brave and redefine the connotation of free, home, and brave. This is a storm too big to fail, which has just fallen. This is that storm. Praise God I have been weatherized before the storm takes place for those who have not headed the messenger are about to experience the life and time of Noah.

Yet, they did not listen to him either and they all perished because of it. Lives of everyone not on the ark died. Everyone not covered by the ark fell and drowned of their ignorance and pride. Everyone who exalted himself or herself above the Great I Am regulates himself or herself, beneath the dirt of the earth. Everyone called upon the name of the Lord is safe and those called upon their selves were lost.

Where are you today? What is your disposition? What is your track? What is your purpose? What is your name? Who is your guide? Who can save you in the midst of the storm, if you do not know the name of the storm master, and he does not know your name? Who are you in this moment? Are you willing to change courses? I can no longer pray for you by direct order from the one above, yet, I would strongly pray for myself in this moment if I feel the winds slowly beginning to beat against my back. We all get a feeling when what appears real is not so real. This is that time and we are in that moment.

I have stocked up on my needs. I am fit for the storm. Covered by the storm master's steady hands through the midst of the storm is a promise to remain obedient, submissive, and faithful heirs. I am ready to ride the waves. I am a part of the great I AM, and nothing destroys the great I AM. I am living in his glory and his purpose, which means he has provided his provisions to sustain the storm. I pray it not last long and not for you, but for his children that have been bounded to you. I pray for redemption and I pray for peace of all.

Just like blessings, redemption comes in many forms and we often do not recognize the truth until after the storm has been in full force in effect for a long time. Longevity is both a blessing and a curse, what will it be for you?

I see a storm coming to a future near you! Welcome to the storm.

This page is intentionally left blank.

If you can believe it and speak to it then you can receive it! A collection thought of experiences realized.

How on Earth Did This Happen?

June 8, 2010

Have you ever taken a moment to review your life and survey how it developed along the journey?

I mean have you ever looked at your choices and thought how each choice led to a different chain reactionary choice. I am referring to those decisions we make we believe are our decisions along to make. You know the ones starting out going one direction and before you know it, they have you doing a topsy-turvy loop into a completely different direction. I mean a type of decision that says this world is mine and I can do with it what I please, as I please without a counter reaction.

You know the decision that always, always, always comes back to wake you up to reality. The decision you believed at the time was the right decision only to find out later it appears to be the wrong decision.

I am referring to the decision that says, how on Earth did this happen. I love these types of decisions. It is the decision, which speaks I know everything I need to know about the situation, the person, the relationship, the thing, the action, or the _____ to make this decision. A decision that says this decision is actually a decision if not made will be the decision I always regret I failed to make. A decision affirming your royalty as a king, as the king, my decision is final. A decision that says no one has the right to question my decision, because no one carries the weight of the decision if it fails or if it succeeds. It is after all...my decision and my kingdom! Therefore, in affect the decision made is mine and mine alone. If it fails, it falls on my head. If it succeeds, it rises above my land. It is my decision.

Have you ever really dissected one of these decisions? I mean have you taken the initial decision to do this or that and place it under a microscope. Have you laid it out on the lab table and just reviewed the entire revisionary process. Have you examined the decision from beginning to end? Have you reviewed the genetic make-up of the conception of the decision way back when the decision first began? Have you taken that decision and placed it in your hands; and when you placed it in your hands did you roll it around in between your fingers to feel where it bent and where it split. Have you looked at that decision and felt the rivers run down its core? Have you inspected the decision for holes, leaks, or trap doors?

I mean have you truly backtrack, the decision from end-result to initial concept. Have you taken that decision and looked it over once or twice. Afterwards did you put it down for a while; then picked it back up and peruse it for a second or third glance. Did you put it down and walked away from it for a while; then come back to the decision and looked it over again? Did you then walked away again; then looked it over from a distance; then finally come back to the decision and slide it under the microscope for further inspection. *What did you see?*

Did the decision look as solid as the first time you made the decision, or was it starting to breakdown? Did the decision hold up to the light? What I mean is when the light came on, how did the decision's truth make you feel on the inside? Did the decision stand the test of time? What I mean by this is did the decision after time passed, still stand as the right decision? Did the decision fall out as you had originally envisioned it in the beginning? I mean each of us when we make a decision have a vision of the outcome of said decision. Each of us when we make a decision should at least survey a brief overview of the decision to completion. *We should.*

How did the decision look, now? Was the right decision? Was it the true decision? Was it the designed decision? Did anyone fall, because of the decision? Did anyone rise, because of the decision? Did everyone survive the decision? Did anyone die, because of the decision? Was anyone born, because of the decision? Did the decision fail or did it succeed in its true purpose? Do you know what the true purpose was by the time the outcome of the decision had arrived? Or, did the decision's purpose get lost in the midst of reaching the outcome? What was the decision? Do you remember? I mean, we often make one decision not realizing in reality that it is not the decision we are making, but a cover for the true decision.

I decided not to go to work today. Why, did I decide, because I was sick, tired, lazy, or just because I wanted to hang out and do my own thing? I decided to leave home and not say a word to anyone. Did I do it, because I was afraid, lonely, depressed, weak, healthy, strong, sick, or was I simply too immature to realize the potential outcome of my decision? Who knows the true answer, but it is in the dissection of the decision that the Truth will reveal itself...*if I seek it.*

I decide to murder my sister. Did I do it because of jealousy, pain, money, hope, denial, or self-interest? Maybe I decided to do it for love or maybe I decided to do it for hate. Who knows, but the truth is in the examination of the conception of the decision.

I decided to do many different things in my life and at each turn, decision resulted. At each turn a decision resulted, which caused an equally reactionary decision to formulate by someone else or me. Whose decision was the controlling decision; their decision or my decision? Whose decision should carry more weight; the initial decision or the final decision? Whose decision got the ball rolling so to speak? Whose decision if not made would have set off a completely different set of decisions? Whose decision started the smoke that led to the fire? Whose decision started the water that caused the flood? Whose decision said, I am lion and hear me roar? Whose decision says this is my household and as such my rules are Law and what I say goes? *Who played God?*

Who took God's power and said you no longer have reign here? Who took God's power and stated emphatically that God did not know what was right by going against what God had already ordained? Who took God's power and said this is no longer your land, but mine? Who took God's power and stated I understand you spoke and the world came into existence, but I no longer need your Word? Who took God's power and said, God I love you, but I need to do this on my own? Who took this decision and said God your power is supreme. Yet, I need to make this decision, because you just cannot see this is the right decision? Who would be so arrogant? Who would decide they knew better than Jehovah Jireh did. Who took God's power and said, God, you sit this one out and let me take the handles for a while? Who took God's power, which he gave for his purpose, and said not this time God this is my time to shine? Who took God's power and said I am woman and hear me roar?

Who decided to change the course of history without consulting with the history-maker? Who took life and brought death? Who took hope and brought despair? Who took peace and brought turmoil? Who took joy and brought pain? Who took Truth and brought fiction? Who took serenity and brought the lack of divinity? Who took God and brought Satan? Who took you and brought me? Who took family and brought stranger? Who took sunshine and brought clouds? Who took a clear day and brought a stormy night? Who lost control and brought chaos? Who can fix it all? *God is who.*

I began with asking, have you ever made a decision in which you had to ask, "How on Earth did this happen?" We have considered many different train-of-thoughts on the decision. Yet, we have not delved into the Truth of this statement. Let us take a moment now that we have dissected the decision to find out what resides under the surface. First, why did we make the decision in the first place? I mean, why did we who are finite make a decision for the infinite God? Second, what were we considering when we decided we knew better than God did in the first place? Was it personal motivation or a spiritual dedication? Third, who knows all, sees all, and does all? Whom are we kidding when we make arbitrary decisions? Do we think that God cannot tell that we usurped his plan? Do we think that God will placate us indefinitely? What are we thinking? Why did we not consider this or talk to God before making the decision? How do we rectify the decision, we ask our self? *Answer: We cannot, but God can!*

We stop taking God's role as supreme King and take our role as supreme prince or princess. We stop driving the bus. We pull over and step out of the driver's seat. We freely give up control to the only one knowing the way in the first place; after all, he drafted the blue prints long before we graced this Earth. We admit each of us plays but a small role in God's historical masterpiece crafted by his hands, his Words, his heart, his Son, and his Spirit. We admit God is the dominant force of all, through all, and for all. We admit our actions may have been the result of faulty logic or emotional haste, but if we acknowledge them, turn them over to God, he is there to absolve us of them all. We admit our purpose is never greater than God's purpose. We admit life is not ours to do and say as we wish regardless of our position or status. We admit each of us walks this Earth only by the grace of our Father up in heaven. We admit life will throw us lemons sometimes, but God makes the best lemonade known to man, woman, or child; *and it is free.*

We just have to receive it, walk in it, live by it, and trust in it. We admit we are frightened of the unknown. We admit we are terrified of the future. We admit we just do not believe we have what it takes to carry out the Master's plan...then we stop trying. We cannot carry out the plan if we wanted to in the first place. We admit we might fall, but failing and being a failure are not the same. We admit the minute we say yes to God, he said my child, "it is well with my soul...welcome home; and what have you learned?"

What have you learned? Do you even know yet? While you decide, here is what I have learned:

I am a child of God.

I am a member of a royal priesthood.

I am a King's child.

I am more than a conquer.

I am free in Christ Jesus.

I am a bold savior, deliverer, and healer.

I am the head and not the tail.

I am a lender and not a borrower.

I am a leader and no longer a follower.

I am a solider for God.

I am a Warrior for Christ.

I am his rightful heir.

I am above and not below.

I am over ties to this world.

I am available for God.

I know this one brings pause.

I am fearless.

In God rests, no fear and I rest in God.

I am more than the world tells me I am.

I am not who I say I am.

I am not who I made myself to be.

Greater is HE that is in me than he that is in the World.

God constructed me by his own hands, Words, and Spirit.

Nothing can separate me from the love of God.

My actions cannot condemn me.

My Words can and most often do by the walk.

Christ lives in me and I live in him.

I can defeat all things through Christ who strengthens me.

I have defeated all things through Christ who strengthens me...they just do not know it yet, but time will reveal the mystery I seek and they discover!

Yet, trust, in time they will.

My ties are now in heaven with my Father.

The things of this world are useful.

Yet, they are not required.

I have lived a full life and it just got fuller.

I have lived a short life and it just got shorter.

I have lived a long life and it just got longer.

I have lived a Godly life and it just got bigger.

I have lived a selfish life and it just got selfless.

I have live a mean-spirited life and it just got gracious.

I have lived a closed life and it just got open.

I have lived a shameful life and it just got shameless.

I have lived a life full of regrets and it just got secure.

I have lived a life without God and it just got Jesus.

I have lived a life on the run and it just got a rest.

I have lived a life in the bushes and it just got a hedging.

I have trusted God when I could trust no one else;

In trusting God, I have prevailed.

I have trusted God when I could not trust myself;

In trusting God, I have prevailed.

I have trusted God when I could not trust my mother;

In trusting God, I have prevailed.

I have trusted God when I could not trust my earthly father;

In trusting God, I have prevailed.

I have trusted God when I could not trust my sister;

In trusting God, I have prevailed.

I have trusted God when I could not trust my brother;

In trusting God, I have prevailed.

I have trusted God when I could not trust my aunt:

In trusting God, I have prevailed.

I have trusted God when I could not trust my uncle;

In trusting God, I have prevailed.

I have trusted God when I could not trust my cousin;

In trusting God, I have prevailed.

I have trusted God when I could not trust my wife;

In trusting God, I have prevailed.

I have trusted God when I could not trust my husband;

In trusting God, I have prevailed.

I have trusted God when I could not trust my best friend;

In trusting God, I have prevailed.

I have trusted God when I could not trust my other friends;

In trusting God, I have prevailed.

I have trusted God when I could not trust my employer;

In trusting God, I have prevailed.

I have trusted God when I could not trust my co-workers;

In trusting God, I have prevailed.

I have trusted God when I could not trust my school

officials;

In trusting God, I have prevailed.

I have trusted God when I could not trust the internet (Face

Book);

In trusting God, I have prevailed.

I have trusted God when I could not trust the establishment;

In trusting God, I have prevailed.

I have trusted God when I could not trust the system;

In trusting God, I have prevailed.

I have trusted God when I could not trust my food;

In trusting God, I have prevailed.

I have trusted God when I could not trust you;

In trusting God, I have prevailed.

I have trusted God when I could not trust her;

In trusting God, I have prevailed.

I have trusted God when I could not trust God;

In trusting God, I have prevailed.

I have trusted God when I could not trust them;

In trusting God, I have prevailed.

I have trusted God when I could not trust us;

In trusting God, I have prevailed.

I have trusted God when I could not trust the collective;

In trusting God, I have prevailed.

I have trusted God when I could not trust the detective;

In trusting God, I have prevailed.

I have trusted God when I could not trust the officer;

In trusting God, I have prevailed.

I have trusted God when I could not trust the teacher;

In trusting God, I have prevailed.

I have trusted God when I could not trust the preacher;

In trusting God, I have prevailed.

I have trusted God when I could not trust the student;

In trusting God, I have prevailed.

I have trusted God when I could not trust the Dean;

In trusting God, I have prevailed.

I have trusted God when I could not trust the Vice

President;

In trusting God, I have prevailed.

I have trusted God when I could not trust the President;

In trusting God, I have prevailed.

I have trusted God when I could not trust my home;

In trusting God, I have prevailed.

I have trusted God when I could not trust the church;

In trusting God, I have prevailed.

I have trusted God when I could not trust the neighbors;

In trusting God, I have prevailed.

I have trusted God when I could not trust anyone;

In trusting God, I have prevailed.

I have trusted God when I could not trust everyone;

I have trusted God when I could not trust my mind;

In trusting God, I have prevailed.

I have trusted God when I could not trust my sight;

In trusting God, I have prevailed.

I have trusted God when I could not trust my hearing;

In trusting God, I have prevailed.

I have trusted God when I could not trust my smell;

In trusting God, I have prevailed.

I have trusted God when I could not trust my taste;

In trusting God, I have prevailed.

I have trusted God when I could not trust my water supply;

In trusting God, I have prevailed.

In trusting God, I have prevailed. I have trusted God when

I simply could not trust;

In trusting God, I have prevailed.

I have trusted God when I truly did not trust God;

In trusting God, I have prevailed.

I have trusted God when I could not trust my anointing;

In trusting God, I have prevailed.

I have trusted God when I could not trust your anointing;

In trusting God, I have prevailed.

I have trusted God when I could not trust my voice;

In trusting God, I have prevailed.

I have trusted God when I could not trust your voice;

In trusting God, I have prevailed.

I have trusted God when I could not trust your body;

In trusting God, I have prevailed.

I have trusted God when I could not trust your touch;

In trusting God, I have prevailed.

I have trusted God when I could not trust your smell;

In trusting God, I have prevailed.

I have trusted God when I could not trust your taste;

In trusting God, I have prevailed.

I have trusted God when I could not trust your vision;

In trusting God, I have prevailed.

I have trusted God when I could not trust my vision;

In trusting God, I have prevailed.

I have trusted God when I could not trust your dreams;

In trusting God, I have prevailed.

I have trusted God when I could not trust my dreams;

In trusting God, I have prevailed.

I have trusted God when I could not trust who you stated

you were;

In trusting God, I have prevailed.

I have trusted God when I could not trust who I stated I

was;

In trusting God, I have prevailed.

I have trusted God when I could not trust your beliefs;

In trusting God, I have prevailed.

I have trusted God when I could not trust my beliefs;

In trusting God, I have prevailed.

I have trusted God when I could not trust your home;

In trusting God, I have prevailed.

I have trusted God when I could not trust my own;

In trusting God, I have prevailed.

I have trusted God when I could not trust your family;

In trusting God, I have prevailed.

I have trusted God when I could not trust my family;

In trusting God, I have prevailed.

I have trusted God when I could not trust your heart;

In trusting God, I have prevailed

.

I have trusted God when I could not trust my heart;

In trusting God, I have prevailed.

I have trusted God when I could not trust your love;

In trusting God, I have prevailed.

I have trusted God when I could not trust my love;

In trusting God, I have prevailed.

I have trusted God when I could not trust your truth;

In trusting God, I have prevailed.

I have trusted God when I could not trust my truth;

In trusting God, I have prevailed.

I have trusted God when I could not trust your walk;

In trusting God, I have prevailed.

I have trusted God when I could not trust my walk;

In trusting God, I have prevailed.

I have trusted God when I could not trust your talk;

In trusting God, I have prevailed.

I have trusted God when I could not trust my talk;

In trusting God, I have prevailed.

I have trusted God.

I have praised God.

I have cried before God.

I have laughed with God and at God.

I have died before God.

I have lived before God.

I have yelled at God.

I have sung before God.

I have written about God.

I have felt like hating God.

I have loved God.

I have realized who was God.

I have bowed down before God.

I have stood up behind God.

I have risen with God.

I have soared alongside God.

I have been in God.

I have smelled God.

I have heard God.

I have tasted God.

I have felt God.

I have reached God.

I have succumbed to God.

I have played with God.

And, he has played with me.

I have lost battles without God.

I have watched victories with God.

I have won the War with God.

I have won my claim to martyrdom for God.

I have become the like image of God.

I have rested with God.

And, God has given me rest.

I have lost everything meaning anything to me.

I have lost myself.

I have lost my home.

I have lost my job.

I have lost perception of my family.

I have lost my deception of the truth.

I have lost my hope.

I have lost my joy.

I have lost my peace.

I have lost my false image of self.

I have lost my sense of connection.

I have lost my sense of disconnection.

I have lost my sense of love.

I have lost my sense of trust.

I have lost my need to please.

I have lost my need to belong.

I have lost my need to be anything other than me.

I have lost them, him, and her.

I have lost us and me.

I have lost others altogether.

I have lost it all.

I have lost my sanity.

I have lost my addictive behavior.

I have lost my need to control.

I have lost my need to dictate the Master's Plan without the

Master.

I have lost my need to live life on the World's terms.

I have lost.

I have lost my belief in people.

I have lost my belief in *you*.

I have lost my belief in me.

I have lost my belief in *God*.

I have lost my belief in heaven.

I have lost my belief in a semblance of *hell*.

I have lost my belief in life.

I have lost my belief in *death*.

I have lost my belief in sorrow.

I have lost my belief in *depression*.

I have lost my belief in regression.

I have simply lost my belief.

I have found my God.

I have found my voice.

I have found my purpose.

I have found my legs.

I have found my arms.

I have found my hands.

I have found my lips.

I have found my eyes.

I have found my smell.

I have found my taste.

I have found my heart.

I have found my progression.

I have found my oppressor.

I have found my deliverer… it lives in me.

I have found my King…he lives in me.

I have found my Queen…she lives in me.

I have found my Messiah…it lives in me.

I have found my redeemer…it lives in me.

I have found my Master…it lives in me.

I have found my tribe…they live in me.

I have found my future…it begins in me.

I have found my joy…it was hidden in me.

I have found my peace… it was buried in me.

I have found my love… it was trapped in me.

I have found my hope… it rests in me.

I have found my life… it is secure in me.

I have found all I need… in me!

I have traveled many roads. I have taken many paths along some very dark alleys. I have climbed many mountains. I have sailed many waves. I have caught many bad apples. I have reached many fertile lands. I have decided to quit a few times. I have decided to start again even more. I have fought the good fight. I have overcame, the long race. I have walked the long journey with only God by my side. I have joined the King at his throne after dethronement. I have eaten at the Lord's Table. *Taste and see how good and perfect the Lord is to me.*

I have sat alongside the Master's tutor. I have learned from his gentle and skillful hands. I have reached levels I never thought existed, which were easier than reaching them without recognizing their endless possibilities. I have and I am, because of the Great I AM. I have reigned during, after, and as-a-result of the storm.

What was your decision?

What did you learn?

What have you lost?

What have you found?

What have you achieved?

What have you defeated?

What have you become?

What have you decided this time?

What have you reached and received?

What have you given up?

What are you prepared to lose to gain what you want and/or need?

What is your truth and does it align with God's Truth?

What is it to you to gain the whole world and lose your soul?

Have you reached the place where God can have the wheel?

If so, let go and let God.

If so, trust God and not man.

If so, believe God's Spirit and not your mine.

If so, live out your faith in action and not words.

If so, speak those things that are not as though they were.

If so, say yes to God and no to self.

If so, stop fearing ... period.

If so, say I can do all things in Christ who strengthens me, and then do.

If so, live out a life honoring God and not self-motivations.

If so, release the past, but remember the lesson, and walk towards the future behind God instead of in front of him.

If so, then the time is now.

If so, then the day is today.

If so, then the hour is at-hand.

If so, then the decision is already made, just accept it, receive it in its entirety, and believe God for the rest.

If so, then God must be in control no matter what comes.

If so, then God is King.

If so, then being small is how God becomes bigger.

If so, then leaving safety is the only way to security.

If so, then reaching the top means letting go of the bottom.

If so, then the lessons learn is ineffectual unless it changes the direction, choices, and purpose of life on God's terms.

Therefore, have you ever wondered how on Earth did this happen. I did. I thought about all my choices. I thought about all my decisions. I thought about all my mistakes. I thought about all my defeats. I thought about my life. I thought about my future. I thought about my stance. I thought about my disposition. I thought about my agenda. I thought about my truth. I thought about my lies. I thought about my fiction. I thought about my separation. I thought about my connection. I thought about my recollection. I thought about all I was. I thought about all I became. I thought about all that I am. I thought about it all. It occurred to me, where was God in it all. *If he was the head then how did I end up here?*

Was it by design or by fluke? Was it by predestination or selective pre-selection? Did it occur, because of the freedom to open or closed the discussion to anyone, but myself? Who knows but God in the end, right?

Here is what I can tell you, in this moment: Trust God, live by his Word, walk in his path, honor the words he give you, love his people, do his will, and all things lost will be found when you are ready to receive what the Lord has prepared for you.

Are you ready? Do you know what that means? Can you handle the road ahead? Do you want to try? What will you decide or have you learned yet, it is not your decision to make, but God's decision?

How on Earth did I end up here?

What is your final answer?

The King awaits your response, check with him before you give it!

Truth exists only in him and through him.

If the answer remains the same after consultation with the designer…stop talking…start living it out!

Amen, the King has spoken, and the time for action is now!

Jesus answered, "I am the way and the truth and the

life. No one comes to the Father except through me.

John 14:6

This page is intentionally left blank.

Living Life on God's Terms

June 10, 2010

Living life on God's Terms is a concept thrown around more often than people tip their server after a good meal. We say it like it is a simple and easy thing to accomplish of our own feat. We consider it a mundane task. We believe that it is a simple process. We believe that things on God's terms are simplistic. We consider things handled on God terms are typical protocol.

We see living life on God's terms as the natural order of things. We consider not living on God's terms as a direct affront to who we are. We consider living life on God terms requires more than we are willing to provide any given day. We forsake God and ourselves to live life as we dictate instead of simply living life on God's terms.

Whose life are we living in the first place? Whose life are we carrying within us to begin with-in the first place? Whose life are we playing with? Whose life is it resting in our vessels?

Whose life is demands supremacy? Whose life is it that creates the need for breathe to enter and exit our body? Whose life is it walking upon this earth? Whose life is it manifested by itself in our love, our affection, our deep desire for a connection, our right to protection, and our hope of reflection?

Whose life is it mandating a change of action? Whose life is it regulating the spiritual realm? Whose life is it living within every being upon the earth? Whose life is it controlling your actions, my actions, or their actions? Whose life is it, which confirms our right to seek an intimate and personal relationship with Christ? Whose life is it that says I can, when everything around me says I cannot? Whose life is it that says I am more than a conqueror even when I am conquered or am I? Whose life states I am more than I appear to be, whether anyone acknowledges it openly or not? Whose life is it requiring a connection to something greater than us? Whose life is sacrificed as an offering in order for us to live? *Whose life is it?*

Is it our life to play games with as if it did not come with a price? Is it our life to treat how we wish? Is it our life to abuse? Is it our life to forsake? Is it our life to take? Is it our life to undo? Is it our life to rewind? Is it our life to fast forward? Is it our life to pause? Is it our life to start? Is our life to stop? Is it our life to alter? Is it our life to mismanage? Is it our life to dangle off a cliff? Is it our life to wreck? Is it our life to freeze or burn? Is it our life to change? Is it our life to sever from the rest of humanity? Is it our life to offer up to anyone, but God? Is it our life to sell? Is it our life to trade? Is it our life to bargain with as if it was some piece of meat on the local corner? *Is it our life?*

I have had a great deal of time to consider these questions and many more. I have thought long and hard about the possible answers. I have gone over in my head on numerous occasions about the ramifications of each complete trail of thought. I have played with the tenets of each. I have done an overview of the compliments to each. I have considered what the Truth of these answers might mean to humanity as a whole and me. I often set alone in my room, my car, my bed, my head, and my natural selected setting of the moment and pondered the potential implications of the mysteries in the questions. *I have.*

So now we have asked the question eventually there must be an answer, *right*? Let us consider the foundational questions. Whose life is it in the first place? Is it our life? Have you considered the implied Truths of the answers? **Yes.** It is God's life in the first place. It is not our life. If these two Truths are relevant for all of humanity than the next Truth becomes how do we manage to mess everything up.

We forget whose life it is. We forget whose temple it is. We forget God created us for his perfect will and not our own. We forget we are here to serve God and not ourselves. We forget this land may be our land, but it is God's universe. We forget you are and I am nothing without God. We forget who we is designed by

God and maintained by God. We forget God's hope in us is not related to anything to do with us, but his desire to bring beauty in a dreary place. We forget God alone, is God and no one nor nothing can alter who he is today, tomorrow, and forevermore. We forget we are not God. We forget God picks and chooses who he wants to carry out his Master plan. We forget 1God can give as quickly as he takes. We forget for every door closes God has already prepare three more to open. We forget life without God is no life at all. It is actually hell. We forget I am created in the image of God. We forget what that means in its inherent connotation. We forget that I am a child of God. We forget the role of a child and the role of a parent. We forget we are a royal priesthood. We forget our Chief Priest.

We forget our place, and so we lose it. We forget our position, and so he gives it to someone else. We forget our station in life, and so it is emptied. We forget our household, and so it is destroyed, by our inability to maintain it as God intended. We forget our land, and so it becomes barren. We forget our fields, and so, sharecroppers take over it when we are not looking. We forget our love, and so it is lost. We forget our family, and so it is broken. We forget our future, and so we return to the past. We forget our destiny, and so he gives it to someone who remembers. We forget our structure, and so it is dismantled. We forget our fireplace, and so the fire burns out. We forget our jobs, and so we lose them. We forget our husbands, wives, partners, lovers, and "friends with benefits" and so someone else finds them. I confess, never understood the whole "friends with benefits," but this new age appears to live there, so it is included. We forget our thoughts, and so they are stolen. We forget our God, and so we cannot find him when he speaks. We forget our church, and so it fails.

We forget our community, and so it deteriorates. We forget our school, and so we become ignorant to the challenges of society. We forget our place, and so we lose it. We forget our heart, and so it hardens. We forget our voice, and so it is given to someone who will speak. We forget our charge, and so we are discharged. We forget our relief, and so we wilt. We forget our joy, and so we have turmoil. We forget our peace, and so the storm over takes us, in the midst of the Master's hand. We forget our life, and so it becomes death. *We forget.*

I did. Many before me have and many after me will. It is what we do when we do not know whose life it is. When you come to understand your life is not your own you, come to understand how your decisions are limited. You recognize your choices are to either obey or rebel. It becomes simple. You can choose to listen to the voice of God and follow his direction or you choose not to submit to his will. There are no other choices to be made by you. This is not to say other choices are not made, because they are, but they are not your choices, they are his.

It took me thirty-four years, approximately forty-four days, and sixteen hours to realize this Truth. *How long will it take you?*

For many who do not know me I often utilize you as a "collective" word. It is not anyone specific. I have a friend that loves to ask me, who? I have to tell you the words "who and whom" has become a yoke around God's children necks. Who is this referring too? Who is that referring too? Who was that about? Who is this about? Who started that project? *Who do you say I am?*

I have learned the quickest way to God's Truth is not in the, "who," but in the where am I in this?

When I began to stop looking for answers outwardly and began looking for the Truth inwardly, God began to become real again, to me. He was always real, but my fascination with you and everybody else displaced the focus from him to me. I became all he was trying to be, which meant there was no room for him. Have you ever usurped God's position? If so, what were your results? Did they fair better than mine? Depending on the stage of this publication, you perhaps know how my life faired. *If not, here is a brief summation.*

I was born in an impoverish community. I grew up with better than most means. I have two parents that made every attempt to love me as best as they knew how with the skills they had at the time. One lives on earth and the other in heaven. I lived a life constantly searching for more than what I appeared to be inwardly and outwardly. I excelled in almost everything I attempted and I was not afraid to attempt anything.

I was so afraid of failure I allowed my fear to control my actions. I was so disconnected from my family I sought out drugs, alcohol, and people to fill then feel the void. I was everything and nothing all at the same time. I was an overachiever. I was striving to reach the top by any means necessary. I was the splitting image of what society stated an African American Black Lesbian should be. *I lived up to it.* I was the product of my environment. I was the summation of my relationships, because I did not develop my own. I was everyone and no one. I was hope full of inwardly despair. I lived to maintain, yet, feared the possibilities of not. I was a child living in an adult body. I was mature beyond my ages, but emotionally immature. I was so many things. Some of them were great and others were not so great. Yet, they were all me and I regret none of them.

I was a thief. I was a cheat. I was you and I was me. I was everything. I was a child of God who had forgotten their place within the kingdom. I lost it all in the matter of seven days. I lost my mind. I lost my home. I lost two jobs within thirty days of each other. I lost my partner of nine years. I lost my mother of thirty-four years. She lives, but she is dead to me today in this moment as I write the whispers of God told from my perspective. I lost my family of thirty-four years. They live today, but they are dead to me now. I lost friends I trusted and friends I did not. I lost hope in people. I lost trust in people. I lost faith in people. I lost my idea of a future. I lost my career track. I lost my educational track. I lost another home within sixty days of the first move. I am homeless, today. *Like I said, I lost it all.*

Yet, I gained so much. I gained my voice. I gained my sight. I gained my heart. I gained my legs. I gained my hands. I gained my being. I gained me. I gained my identity. I gained my serenity. I gained a definition of truth and Truth. I gained my life. I gained my freedom. I gained my victory. I gained my reward. I gained my place of peace living buried deep inside of me. I gained my source and he never fades or becomes weary. I gained a new sense of purpose. I gained my reality. I gained my spirituality. I gained value. I gained vision. I gained a mission. I gained a connection to something greater than myself. I gained my inner person. I gained all I had been prior, but ran away from so many times in my immaturity.

I gained, Jesus. I gained, God. I gained the Holy Spirit. I gained the Trinity. I gained Jehovah Jireh. Trust me on this one, he has provided every need that came, I have not lacked. I do not lack. I may struggle, but struggling is not lacking. Learn the difference and live the Truth.

So whose life is it? I found my answer. What is yours?

I know what it is to be in need, and I know what it is to have plenty. I have learned the secret of being content in any and every situation, whether well fed or hungry, whether living in plenty or in want. Philippians 4:12

This page is intentionally left blank.

If You Conform to Anything, You Will Fall for Everything

July 17, 2010

If you conform to anything then you will fall for just about everything. Have you ever considered what it cost to be successful? I mean have you thought about the long hours, the lonely nights, the sleepless days, and the restless spirits. Most people are not successful, because they focus on the journey to success instead of the rewards in-between the hurdles towards the end to victory. If I thought about how long the road was, I might take a snapshot and call it a day. When I think about the hope, joy, peace, trials, tribulations, strength, character built, baggage lost, and wholeness found, I see a life of possibilities instead of a world of possible defeats. I have never known a person living in defeat unless they stopped living.

Defeat like success is defined by what we do and not what we say, right? Perhaps not says the man who spoke a word of prosperity and found a job. Perhaps so says the man who got off the couch and in the mall to fill out applications for a job. How you define a thing will determine if that thing rules you; or you rule it. I cannot live a life rooted in fear and expect God to show me his mighty power. For out of many will come one.

I searched scripture and found no reference of fear producing faith. I searched my heart and find no place where fear rules my thoughts. I searched your words and fear kills your life and had begun to reshape mine.

Therefore, your fear is no longer privy to my space and my space is no longer accepting of your fear. Faith comes by hearing and reading the word of God. Yet, belief of the unseen can only be accomplished by performing the hope and manifestation of the present and future. For faith without works is just as dead as a spirit without God.

Sometimes assimilation requires a reduction or complete loss of self. To assimilate requires a loss of self-identity. It requires a loss of self-perseverance in order to conform to what is on the table. You learn to leave what you like behind in order to meet the current needs of the day. I say if I must conform to anything to have everything I desire than I am seeking the wrong desires. You should never have to conform to anything in order to have your basic needs, wants, and desires. If you come across a path and the choice is between success and failure choose success. However, if the choice is between self and others – always choose self.

I have learned in life choosing others over your basic need to survival means you conform to anything, thus, you fall for everything. I would rather fall for nothing and retain my self-respect, my self-identity, and my self-love. I would rather be homeless and love myself than rich on money and broke on spirit. I would rather be sick of loneness than healthy on superficial companionship.

If you will conform to anything then you have just falling for everything. What does such an individual look like? Is it the brother on the street driving his new Lexus he cannot afford to pay for any more than the first two months? Is it the sister in the hair salon buying her self-worth instead of showing it from within? Is it you who just stopped to read this poem and saw more of yourself than I saw of me?

For everything you fall for be sure you have a reason to explain the fall. Sometimes we fall for the words out of their mouths. Sometimes we fall for the step in their walk. Sometimes we fall for the caress of their tongue. Sometimes we fall for the dip in their hip. Sometimes we simply fall, because they fell. Sometimes we fall to see if they will pick us up. Sometimes we fall to keep them down. Sometimes we fall to release the hounds. Sometimes we fall to pick up the children. Sometimes we fall, because before you can rise, you have to fall.

If you will conform to anything then you have just falling for everything. It is said to know thy self is to know God.

However, if you know God, but say you do not know yourself then how can you know God? For if I am against everything and nothing then where do you begin and where do I end? Live today like it was tomorrow and you live tomorrow like it was today. My future is not a by-product of your thoughts. My future is the by-product of my dedication in God, my commitment to my future, and our collective journey towards them both.

I do not conform to anything that has not been validated by something. God does not assimilate his plans into man's plan so why do his children? Are you a child of God or a chameleon of the world? When you find the answer, seek the Truth by living it and instead of speaking it!

For God has not given us the spirit of fear; but of power, and of love, and of a sound mind. 2 Timothy 1:17

This page is intentionally left blank.

Not Yet

July 21, 2010

How often do you make your way towards the door only to be informed…not yet?   It is something those who are progressive have a complicated dilemma understanding.

I pose the following:

How many times have you been running late for work and an accident occurred on your regular route.

How many times have you left early and arrived at work for the project that was supposed to go to your second in command?

How many times has a delay now turned out to be a greater reward later?

How many times have you cursed the delay and then blessed the delay when things unseen became things realized.

How many times must God hold you back because the provisions are not in order and if you go forward you go forward without him?

How many times did you go forward after God said no and the cost to go backwards was more than you could afford to pay?

How many times did you wish you had waited only to be told it was too late and the choice had been sealed?

How many times would you say, yes, and Amen, when God says...not yet, my child, if only you could get a glimpse of what was on the other side?

I recall a time when I was in the eighth grade. I was extremely upset with my mother. I had wanted to go to this party that a friend of mine had to be with my new boyfriend. Now, being 14 or 15 years old at the time I was not allowed to date. So this was a secret rendezvous to which mother always knows about in some manner. I pleaded, and pleaded, and she remained firm. Two days later I returned to school to learn my "new boyfriend" had been shot in a drive-by shooting.

I pondered then about how much God knows about what is head of us. I considered the possibility she had an inclination of what was to come that evening, even if she did not know the details, she knew it was not a place for her child. I never openly thanked my mother for her strictness, but I did, often afterwards.

As children, we know so much more than everyone. We know what is best for us. We know the path we should take. We know the friends we should have. We know the mates we should mate with. We know who we hopefully better than everyone. We live a life full of I know better than you. We consume rights like a soft drink. We spout our demands as a two year-old spouts the alphabets for the first time. We know who we are, what we have, and we want it now.

Then there is dad sitting on the throne shaking his head at our impetuous behavior, attitude, and naivety. Dad grafted the plan. Dad wrote the thesis and designed the body of the text. Dad constructed the roadmap through the maze and to the finish line. Dad manufactured the factory that will assemble the pieces into a usable fixture. Dad conceptualized the hypothesis to test the assumptions he knew in advance would registered – true. Only Dad can reduplicate the study of your life and my life. Only Dad has the key to open the door that needs to be open and close the door, which needs to be closed, so why did you decide to leave the key holder.

Sometimes not yet, should be the time for praise and worship instead of a moan and groan moment. If I look over my life, I have many not yet moments and I can trace a greater blessing received later connected to the not yet then would have been realized had the not yet been, proceed as a now.

"And the King will say, 'I tell you the truth, when you did it to one of the least of these my brothers and sisters, you were doing it to me!'

Matthew 25:40

Through adversity I faced my fears, I conquered the

demons of doubt, and God grew bigger in me than I

imagined. Nothing that was lost did he not find. DNB

I Stopped and Wondered

August 3, 2010

I stopped and wondered tonight as I sat in my 10 x 14 bedroom tonight. It is the room I grew up in. It is where I had some of my darkest nightmares and greatest dreams. It is where the Lord rocked me to sleep each night. It is where I first remembered thinking one day I would be more than the color of my skin or the disposition of my sexual identification. I struggled for years with this issue. Yet, time and experience has a way of changing struggles into successes. I stopped and wondered.

I stopped tonight to wonder many things. It occurs to me I have an innate ability in selecting movies or books, which so closely correlate to my own life I wonder if God preordained them so I could feel at ease about the content and context of my own life as I ingested their knowledge and hidden truth. I stopped and wondered.

Tonight, ironically enough I picked up a movie in which yet again life imitated fiction. Except, the movie is actually a true story so for once it was life imitating life and the parallel throughout the movie and this book are so uncanny at moments I had to pause and then poise. Wow! I stopped and wondered.

It occurs to me in many forms of how great God is and can be. He is God. The protagonist of the story, a *Conversation with God* undergoes a series of life altering naturally expected life events. Many of us have or will experience the same events at one point in our life on some scale. He has a horrible car accident while becoming taken by a homeless woman on the corner as he drives his car by and through a four-way intersection. His fault, which leads to a loss of job and then he loses his home. He seeks works, but is unable to find it. Having thought to be healed only to learn his healing was premature. The doctors missed his broken neck. Thus, he is not only prevented from working when he wants to, but he sees his dreams dashed, stamped, and pigeonholed. He sees his life as he knew it forever reconfigured. He is not who he envisioned as a child, this fact is obvious. I stopped and wondered.

The story unfolds. He ends up homeless. He goes to his family home only to sneak into the shed where he finds a tent. Riding on a bus he finds a way to a park. He pitches his tent in the darkness of night. A home for the homeless is what he has now. I stopped and wondered.

Before now it is quite obvious he was a proud man. He was a man of bear minimal middle class stature. This is not who he is today in this new world he finds himself engulfed within as midnight becomes daybreak. He is awoken by the gatekeeper of the transient park. He is now classified as transient. There is a scene where the natives who have been there so long they are native to the land similar to how America sometimes confuses Christopher Columbus as the original settler of North America until we have a history lesson and remember you cannot find or discover something already founded or discovered. I stopped and wondered.

Yet, the native transients cooked up a scrumptious meal of trash can chili left over from someone's lunch, a pack of saltine crackers, sprinkled with a pack of salt and a pack of pepper for added flavoring. The meal of champions, right; wrong, despicable we are the most-wealthiest nation and citizens considered this prime dinner delight. I stopped and wondered.

Our protagonist still fresh from a few good meals passes on the blue plate special. Instead he finds himself at a classier dining spot. The local dumpster behind a classy restaurant and I am literally trying to comprehend the wetness upon my check as I watch this scene. There's heaviness in my heart I cannot understand or invalidate. I am consumed by a weird emotion. There is a strangeness happening in this vessel of God. There are more signs of emotional distress. I tell myself this is a movie. I close my eyes like the small child afraid of the bogeyman as her parents close the door for the fourth time that night. Daddy, please make it go away. It does not; instead I am consumed by tears.

They have a name now. I cannot call them what they are not. My soul aches. I stopped and wondered.

It aches not for the man whose story resembles mine in such an uncanny formulated trip down recent ghost of resurrection past that I pinch myself. It is a tear for each person I met along the way who remains homeless, broken, discarded, deregulated, miss-shelved, or otherwise disjointed from normal society. I mean I could postulate about how I am technically homeless, because this is not my home. Yet, it is a place I rest. I grew up here so this is my family home it is just not *my* home. Yet, it provides comfort in transition. So many people I met are not as blessed. They sleep under bridges in the dark of night and the hot of day. They go from soup kitchen to soup kitchen in hopes of a warm meal. Some have their families and others have none. I stopped and wondered.

About a week ago I saw a woman walking in Texas heat on a July summer day. She had an oversized suitcase resembling that of a duffle bag more than a suitcase. Yet, praises to God, it was upgraded with wheels. She had on all black. She wore a long sleeve button down shirt, underneath was a black t-shirt, accessorized with black corroders pants, and run down black tennis shoes, even the shoestrings were black. I love black, but man this was more than I could take in the moment. Did I mention it was Texas in the summer? I am sure I did, but it bears mentioning again. What I am saying is it was HOT! If the indication of sweat on her brow was not a clue then the look of despair surrounding her persona should have been. I have many stories to tell of my own time in transition. Yet, this is not such a time. I will state, I too was both figuratively and literally homeless not too long ago. So, my heart can now go beyond an ache to a deeper understanding of this woman's current situation to which I am sure she never saw coming. I stopped and wondered.

I digress. I very rarely take this route to church, but by God's design today this is the route I am destined to travel. As I am praising the Lord, which is a customary act I enjoyed en route the Lord in my private worship moment. I prefer to set my own atmosphere before entering his house and I do. It is how I believe we come, ready, and not waiting. I stopped and wondered.

I am driving. She sticks out like Judas as the Homecoming of Jesus Christ. You cannot miss her if you were blind. It is Texas and she is dressed like a member of the Nebuchadnezzar from the Matrix as they rescue Morpheus on a scorching hot Summer day around 2:40 p.m. For those who do not know this is about twenty minutes sly of the hottest time of the day, here. I sweat when I look at her and then I cry on the inside. I have mixed emotions. I am grateful for how God brought me through, yet again and I am sad there are so many still digging through the trash for what should be a basic human right, food. I stopped and wondered.

I can never seem to work towards the conclusion of the story, because the God in me wonders where his children are living out his life upon the earth. How can you receive so many blessings and never be a blessing to others? I get lost in transition. I am lost still. Even in my moments of homelessness I was and am a generous person by nature. After months of no income, almost four to be exact, I treat myself to a wonderful steak dinner. My meal, a tasty appetizer, a perfectly prepared medium rare steak and two great sides, and the best pepper flavored glass of red wine brought me a well-deserved reward of a $55 price tag. It was worth every cent. I stopped and wondered.

My waitress was very attentive. She spoke of her hard times and financial struggles. I kept her at least thirty minutes pass closing. Yet, I never asked for anything. It was as if God knew my trials and tribulations and sent me a special angel to remind me, man may not, but God always rewards his good and faith servants. He did. I stopped and wondered.

I left $155.00 on the table, blessed the meal, my angel, and departed for the evening. I have never wanted for anything in my weakest moment. I have been homeless and yet not penniless. I hold this insatiable desire to please my Lord. Thus, I live my life as I believe he would have me live it...in abundance even when the natural states otherwise. It is because of this consistent and persistent lifestyle I believe I have every need and many of my wants. He has given me charge over a little and I have used the little to make great things out of nothing. Thus, he has given me charge over more and the more he gives the more I return. He keeps giving. I stopped and wondered.

So, I return to the story of the depressed, rejected, and subjected child of God walking on a hot street towards the homeless shelter one steaming hot summer day on a Sunday afternoon in Dallas, Texas. I pass her by like many others have I suspect. Yet, I say without any level of pride, I am not like others.

There is something within me, which causes me to stop abruptly as I get twenty feet pass her struggling to maintain her bag. I make a mental note of the funds in my purse. I figure it is about twenty three or twenty four dollars. I search my heart, which is God in a split second. I hear give all the ones. I never count it, but I pull it out. I make an illegal U-turn in a two lane street. I pull up alongside the woman who appears both slightly confused and full of despair my soul leaps to touch hers. She is asking a fellow homeless man how far is the nearest shelter. I gave blood next to there about twelve or thirteen years ago, when I was going through one of my many character building times of this short life. It is about two blocks away. I stopped and wondered.

I hand her the money. She looks at it as if it is attached to a live snake. Then she looks at me as if I just might be the snake. For a minute I secretly wonder. I am not. I say what I always say in one of these moments, of living out the gospel I have experienced in my life, "God Bless You, and have a Blessed Day." It is my signature saying in one of these moments. I did not accumulate the money, God did. I am just a watch keeper of my portion of his treasure on earth. I stopped and wondered.

I return to this now fear-stricken woman contemplating why a complete and total stranger has provided her with money out of the clear blue in what I gather is a foreign land to her from a general purpose standpoint. I repeat it, "God bless you and have a blessed day." She said, "What made you give me this? You just gave me this out of the clear blue?" My reply, "Yes", to her accusation and astonished question rolled, packed, and tied with a distrustful look all-in-one. I stopped and wondered.

Again, she stares at the snake and the snake giver. I am perplexed. Inwardly, I think to myself, at best it is five dollars and at worst it is three. I have always had little concern for money. I have always been blessed with it in one way or another. At the age of twenty-two for a summer I made an average of $2,000 a week. I let the job go. I thought in my infancy this was a normal occurrence. Yea, figured that one out pretty quick, not what I thought, but we live and we learn. I stopped and wondered.

So, back to my moment of Good Samaritan twilight zone, where I feel like I must of missed something. I am sure the entire communication lasted a whole three minutes max, yet, it felt like an eternity. I have never been sequestered and interrogated for giving money. I was slightly shocked. Again, it was only three to five dollars. My average meal is at least twice that price. When I smoked, my cigarettes were getting close to twice that price. I intentionally leave money in places to surprise myself in amount three or four times that amount. I like surprises, what can I say. A lesson my mother taught me. I get paid, I take money I hide it somewhere and then when needed God reveals where I hide it. I stopped and wondered.

So, in our three minute conversation Tiny Tim's lost reverse mother and I look on at each other. She is at a lost and I confess, I am at a greater lost. It is an act of kindness. It dawns on me, how you can recognize something you have never experienced. I am heartbroken. I stopped and wondered.

Now, as I finally bid her adieu we say our goodbyes and I think at least she will have money to get a bed at the shelter. God sent me where I was needed. Yet, the deeper issue rest in how someone becomes so separated from society they cannot discern an act of kindness as an act of kindness. I shook my head then and I shake my head now in remembrance. I imagine her family. Who are they? Do they care anything about her? Are they out looking for her? Did she flee in the middle of the night from an abusive relationship? What brings her to Dallas, Texas, with nothing more than a suitcase? It gives me pause and then it causes me a deep pain. Where is my God in this? It is in me. It is in others like me. It is in you. It is wherever someone takes a stance against oppression and a stance for human rights. I stopped and wondered.

I am left troubled. I am left wondering if anyone else ever stops to wonder. I stopped to wonder how life could look beyond her and see less than humanity. I stopped and wondered how no one appeared to care and if they did, where were they? Did they have their own share of problems? Where her problems greater than their resources? Perhaps, she chartered out on her own. Maybe, she met a mate and it ended badly. I may never know. I stopped and wondered.

Yet, this I know. No one reacts to an act of kindness with such suspect unless they have been so badly damaged by someone or many some ones close to them. The look in this woman's eyes spoke of betrayal after betrayal. I recognized it. I felt it. Yet, mine appeared to be shielded by a deeper covering in God from an earlier age at least this is what I tell myself. I stopped and wondered.

My heart broke for her despair. I caught a tear as I drove away. I simply stopped and wondered.

New Leader

August 7, 2010

Who is the leader in your life?

There are many aspects of being a leader.

A leader is self-assure.

A leader is wise and leads by wisdom.

A leader is true even when events would navigate weaker

individuals down a different path.

A leader is solid on rocky ground.

A leader is sufficient regardless of an insufficient system.

The leader in me needs to meet the new leader in you.

A leader is confident in spite of their inner insecurities.

A leader is patient through every circumstance.

A leader is knowledgeable beyond what they see, because true leaders are visionaries. And, visionaries lead from the front of the line while others cower behind.

A leader is peace in the midst of a storm.

A leader is forever seeking new inroads as they complete the current course.

A leader may not enjoy the journey, but learns from every rock, peddle, or split in the road.

The leader in me needs to meet the new leader in you.

A leader is a positive force in the electromagnetic field of elevation.

A leader is the coefficient a radioactive field.

A leader is the beacon the group holds on to when things bend from left to right.

A leader is the staple fixture of any entity.

A leader knows who they are by living out it in actions dictated by their words.

A leader seeks the challenge of the situation for purpose of the challenge.

The leader in me needs to meet the new leader in you.

A leader never questions the failure, but investigates the successes to learn how the failure was possible.

A leader can fix a problem better than they can cause a solution to develop into a problem.

A leader is in you.

A leader is in me.

A leader can be developed or revealed.

A leader can be installed or removed.

A leader never faints.

A leader never boasts.

A leader knows their source of strengthen and it does not come from without, but from within.

A leader knows their source.

The leader in me needs to meet the new leader in you.

In the end a leader will seek the path of least resistance in order to achieve the path of greatest gain.

A leader is not set on a path, but committed to the journey's lessons received by journey's end.

A leader may never know they lead anything until the opportunity to recognize its completion is transformed into fruits of labor they never saw form.

Some leaders are born while others are made possible through education and even more are crafted by experiences.

Many leaders will never hold the title of leader, but live the life of a stationary. This is the mark of true leadership.

I have learned being a leader is not in what I say.

I have learned being a leader is not in what you say about me.

I have learned being a leader is not in what

I think.

I have learned being a leader is not in what you think.

I have learned a leader seeks councils from every member of their

team, but trusts the inspiration from above.

The key in life is to learn to control

the inner thoughts of your mind.

Once you learn to control your thoughts

you have conquered the power in your words.

Upon learning to control your words

you learn to navigate your steps towards a God inspired and

perfected path to wholeness.

When you learn to control your steps

you learn to control your fate.

As you control your fate, you learn to control the journey.

Again, this ensures your learning along the journey of life is

achieved through the leader in me as I learn from the leader in you.

The God of your fathers is your safe resting-place, and under you are his eternal arms: driving out the forces of your haters from before you, he said, Let destruction overtake them. Deuteronomy 33:27

This page is intentionally left blank.

Relationships

August 7, 2010

In this world relationships are important.

A relationship improperly formed can make or break you.

A relationship designed by God will surely manifest newness in

your Spirit.

A relationship is the center most important definition of any two

people.

If I am in relation with you then we have a relationship and this

relationship can only be crafted by the contents of the people

involved.

In this world relationships are important.

What are your contents?

Would anyone pair with you?

Would anyone accept you as a positive force?

I am learning that each relationship requires work.

If it be a friendship it still requires work.

If it be a partnership it still requires work.

If it be a love-ship it still requires work.

It all requires work.

What are your contents?

My relationship begins with the one who establishes every good

relationship.

My relationship with others is determined by my relationship with

God.

If I fail to develop a healthy relationship with God then I will fail

at every relationship I enter.

If I fail to learn the true character of God then I will never learn the

true character of anyone else.

I love you means more than saying words.

I love you means more than buying you candy.

I cannot live for God if I do not know how God lives.

I cannot live for God if I reject the God in me.

Relationship is a two-way street, which sometimes curves left to

right.

Relationship is not a sword, but a created puzzle.

My relationships all began with the one who establishes every

good relationship.

Consider a breakdown of the word

Re-lation-ship:

Re – To do over again

Lation – To come together

Ship – An object navigating seas and oceans constructed of

resilient material to weather any storm

Now, consider the reconstruction of the word **Re-lation-ship** *to do over again by bringing together to weather any storm containing resilient material able to navigate seas and oceans.*

Relationship defined and reconstructed, but best lived by example and not by voice.

In this world relationships are important. Chose them carefully, but nourish them with the Love of God and the sprinkle of the Holy Spirit.

Journeys

August 15, 2010

Many Journeys begin without even a clue of possibility or awareness a journey has even begun. People wake up one day and walk out into the world to see two diverting paths. *It is your journey.*

Down one path is a light of spectrum hope and renewal of life. It appears to contain a sense of peace. It appears to recognize the truth in life of this moment. It appears to treat the journeymen as a welcomed addition. It appears. *It is your journey.*

Down the other path is a dark gloomy cloud road of silence. It beckons the quite morning air. It is a place where most look for God and find themselves. It is a place opposite of what is expected when things are least expected. It is, because he is, and we are who he called us to be. *It is your journey.*

It is a journey of love, hope, joy, despair, prosperity, and much more than anyone one person could truly comprehend or undertake without a guiding force. It is a journey meant to build character. It is a journey meant to strengthen your mind. It is a journey meant to fortify your body. It is a journey meant to bring you into your destiny and out of your past. It is a journey of where your dreams are realized and your hopes are fulfilled. *It is your journey.*

In life we go through many journeys. Some of them are pleasant. Some of them are joyous until the bottom drops, the roof caves in, and the walls fall down. It is a life full of mystery and a heart full of missed chances and second time romances. It is a place of peace in the midst of a storm and the place of joy in the day of celebration. It is a journey you pray ends understanding the next one is set to begin. *It is your journey.*

My life has been filled with many journeys. Some have brought joy. Many have held pain. A few have been a part of you, a few a part of me, and a few a part of Dawn. Yet, in them all I am what I could have never been without being tossed into the sea, so I could learn how to swim. It is said only the strong survive. I wonder if they understood this truth:

My strength is defined by my character.

My strength is recognized in my walk.

My strength is confirmed by my actions.

My strength is solidified by my beliefs.

My strength is renewed in each victory.

My strength is displayed in my features.

My strength is controlled by the Creator.

My strength is acknowledged by what you see and not what you hear.

My strength is me and it is a part of you, because each person we touch can either add too or subtract from what we are. *It is your journey.*

Be careful in who you allow into your life. In my journey I realized one thing that carries me through each day. True strengthen comes from those closes to you who remain with you in spite of what they see or what they hear. They become a part of your journey. They become a part of you. They become a part of me. They become, because you are within me. Yet, how do we define what is you and what is me. *It is your journey.*

I stopped trusting in this last journey for a spell. I stopped listening to outside influences for a time. I stopped acknowledging misspoken truths and half spoken lies. I listened with my heart. I listened with my Spirit. I listened with my mind. I listened to the beat of the drum in my body and the sensation in my tongue. I listened to anything, but everything. I listened to who I wanted to be instead of who they stated I was not to become. I simply listened. He heard. She responded. They came through. Who came out is still a work in progress, but I am enjoying the work and the steady growth coming through with it in each passing day. *It is your journey.*

I have gone through life without a care. I have learned to recognize why this matters and why you should care. At every step you take a new person comes into your life. They bring with them their own set of issues. They bring with them their own set of historical challenges in life. They either deposit something with you or take away from you. Sometimes they do both. *It is your journey*, but most are never taken alone.

This is my life. I await my future. I have brief thoughts of my past, but greater hope in my present, because my future holds the key to who God has prepared me, to be in spite of who I appeared as before. I am his child, but I am also his fruit. It is my journey, but I share the road if you are able to help carry the load. *It becomes our journey.*

So riddle me this…if you began a journey alone and you find a team along the way, would you keep the fruit or keep the lessons. I choose to keep who I am and what I learned from within by becoming closer to my heart of who we are and who we should all be in you. *It has become our journey, you, me, and us.*

All the believers were one in heart and mind. No one claimed that any of his possessions was his own, but they shared everything they had. With great power the apostles continued to testify to the resurrection of the Lord Jesus, and much grace was upon them all.

Acts 4:32 - 33

Epilogue

I have learned certain things in my life, which never leave me without a reason to keep pushing through even when I cannot see my way through. This year came as a surprise to me, but never to God. It was through a moment in time, and introspective viewpoint, and an extrovert journey I learned the true meaning of FAITH! Faith is only possible when you envision the impossible and then make it happen.

Born on the wrong side of Dallas for many I suspect, I was birthed with a dream waiting for attainment. It has begun. This is only the beginning of a continuous relationship with my Creator and yours if you will allow him to be. I may not know what the road has in store ahead of me, but I know the one who clears the path.

According to The American Heritage Dictionary, my name Dawn in the second verb definition is *to begin to appear or develop; emerge;* and in the third verb definition *means to begin to be perceived.* This is me and I am a dawn of history.

Currently, I am pursuing my M.Ed. in Higher Education, a MBA, and an Advance Certificate in Conflict Resolution from Dallas Baptist University in Dallas, Texas. I prayerfully speak a graduation date of no later than December of 2011. Yet, I leave the possibility of a God extended detour in this area if additional collegiate training is necessary before release from the university is in ushered in to complete what God has ordained for me to complete in his time and at his direction.

In addition, to other works at different stages of completion, I, the author am herein requesting submissions from other novice, intermediate, experienced, or not writers in the LBGTQ community and friends. It is a vision to publish a collection of works focused on the struggles, belief systems, dichotomy of living homosexual in a heterosexual world, or vice versa, and a coming of age story of who the writer envision themselves to be. The concept of the story should be a basic biography of the writers' early life, adolescent life, young adult years, and current position. The purpose is to show others how they are never alone even if they stay alone. Each of us share similar backgrounds whether we are straight, gay, bisexual, or otherwise, but if we never tell the story, then we continue to see a world of us and them instead of a world made by God, which shelters God's children by their faith and not their sexual identification.

If you are interested please submit your story, poem, or prose to eyhcs2010@gmail.com or P. O. Box 150597, Dallas, Texas 75315. If you would like to retain the exclusive right to your work please forward the submission with payment for registration of $35.00 per work to aforementioned post office box or contact me directly for electronic payment options. Otherwise the work will be copyrighted under Equally Yoked Heavenly Creations Services' trademark with co-rights to the respective author.

This year began a mystery and the future will unfold the question of the mystery. I ask each reader of this book to join me as we discover the mystery together. Simply walk your testimony of truth by living it outwardly instead of inwardly. Honor God and even great tragedies become great rewards, this I can attest to be true in spirit and the law.

About the Author's Year with God

As 2009 came to an end I began to hear whispers from God. They began as dreams and transformed into visions. As the New Year began my heart opened up and God's Spirit flowed through in exponential inspiration.

I saw my deepest beliefs in people, establishments, and self-challenged. My faith and perseverance were tested beyond measures to which I perceived to be humanly possible. My sanity came under question and rightfully so at times. Yet, through it all my God held me as the storms raged, as the ship's anchor lost ground, and as the motor stalled. I rose as the waters receded. This book holds the remnants of the storm and the blessings found in broken pieces of a life rebuilt. The pot of God's gold at the end of the rainbow has redeemed me into who I envisioned myself to be, before the truth of my witness caused me to shift, my reality.

I close with this final thought. For every battle, God has prepared a greater victory. For every lost, God has already provided a greater treasure. Living for God, through Christ, and according to his purpose pays forward the love of Christ in ways you least expect. I have learned to trust God when I could not see clearly enough to know who he appeared as in my life. He is everywhere and nowhere. Angels are truly among us and failure to see the trees amidst the forest may cost your heritage, your witness, and your testimony more than you can afford to pay without heavenly insurance from the Almighty God of alpha and omega.

God is still speaking. I am still listening.

With the Love of Christ,

Dawn Nichelle Boyland

"Through change comes adversity and through adversity we understand our voice is uniquely ours and ours alone"

- D. Nichelle Boyland

eyhcs2010@gmail.com